Richmond upon Thames Libraries

Renew online at www.richmond.gov.uk/libraries

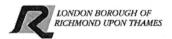

LONDON BOROUGH OF
RICHMOND UPON THAMES

THE NEW SNOBBERY

TAKING ON MODERN ELITISM AND
EMPOWERING THE WORKING CLASS

DAVID SKELTON

Biteback Publishing

First published in Great Britain in 2021 by
Biteback Publishing Ltd, London
Copyright © David Skelton 2021

David Skelton has asserted his right under the Copyright, Designs and Patents Act
1988 to be identified as the author of this work.

ISBN 978-1-78590-657-2

10 9 8 7 6 5 4 3 2 1

A CIP catalogue record for this book is available from the British Library.

Set in Minion Pro and Akzidenz-Grotesk

'Some ideas are so stupid that only the uneducated
can believe them.'

THE OBSERVER, NOVEMBER 2019

'It's time for the elites to rise up against
the ignorant masses.'

FOREIGN POLICY, JUNE 2016

CONTENTS

WHY HAVE I WRITTEN THIS BOOK?

Why did I decide to write this book? And why now? The first reason is very personal. I might not live in Consett any more, but my friends and family do, and I have spent the past few years listening to them being routinely insulted by people who regard themselves as 'progressive' and 'enlightened'. Wrapping up the writing of this book was difficult, because every day brought a new example of (generally, but not always) left-wing people finding new ways to describe the working-class as bigoted or stupid. I saw prejudice against people I care about and places I love become acceptable in so-called 'polite society', in progressive Britain and in parts of the media. The people I know and love who voted for Brexit and (after much soul-searching) voted Tory for the first time in 2019 aren't stupid, bigoted or racist – in every way they're exactly the opposite. The real prejudice is coming from the elitists who use political disagreement as an excuse to throw around snobbish abuse. I'm not prepared to stand back and let my friends and family be insulted in this way; I think it's important that this snobbery is called out for what it is – hence my decision to write this book.

The second reason is political. The years since the Brexit referendum have seen the Tory Party move in the direction I've long been advocating: towards a genuinely One Nation politics that embraces an active state in order to bring about economic renewal to places that badly need it. I don't need to be persuaded of the importance of 'levelling up'. I saw my hometown devastated by the loss of the steelworks that gave it pride and identity, and then be forgotten about by generations of politicians who had simply moved on. I've seen proud work replaced with insecure jobs that provide neither meaning nor dignity. I want this book to be a reminder that working people should not be forgotten any more and that the call they made for change in the referendum of 2016 and the election of 2019 must be responded to with the kind of decisive economic reform that dramatically improves people's quality of life.

Now is a once-in-a-century opportunity to achieve a permanent realignment in British politics, based on a multi-racial, working-class Conservatism, with Conservatism always acting in the interest of workers. Just as my last book, *Little Platoons*, saw the real potential for towns in England's north and the Midlands to set the path towards a Tory majority, this book seeks to suggest the kind of lasting change that would make the realignment of December 2019 into a permanent one. The May 2021 elections, with the Conservatives taking the Hartlepool by-election with a dramatic swing and Labour losing councils as symbolically important as Durham, showed that December 2019 was not a one-off. Now is the time to be bold and deliver the kind of change that voters in Hartlepool and County Durham voted for.

The third reason is about timing. Now that Brexit is done, we have the autonomy and the tools to remake our economy. The grimness of the Covid crisis has shown how significant so-called 'elementary' workers are to the economy and has also illustrated the importance of having a strong manufacturing sector. Post-Brexit and post-Covid presents the opportunity for a remaking of the economy along the lines I set out in this book, where dignity of work is central, working people are respected and represented throughout society and a revived manufacturing base restores pride to towns across the country, as well as creating millions of skilled jobs.

The fourth reason is about what I have learned over the past few years since I wrote *Little Platoons*. I have had the good fortune to be able to see in person what the 'Asian Tigers' – Hong Kong, Singapore, South Korea and Taiwan – were able to do with intelligent industrial policies to create a strong manufacturing base, just as other countries were giving up on industry. This has reaffirmed my view that British policy-makers have had much too narrow horizons for too long. Rather than endlessly trying to relitigate the British political arguments of the 1970s and 1980s, or having pointless arguments about street signs, it is surely about time we looked to those countries who have developed strong manufacturing bases, skilled work and strong communities and see what we can learn from them.

THE BIRTH OF THE NEW SNOBBERY

The 2016 referendum on EU membership marked the first time in generations that the once industrial working class flexed its political muscles and helped to change the direction of the country – against the almost universal advice of the ruling political, business and cultural class. Three years later, the same voters proved pivotal to the result of the 2019 general election, with the so-called Red Wall crumbling and 120 years of class-based partisan loyalties melting away as dyed-in-the-wool Labour voters abandoned the party, handing the Conservatives their biggest majority since Margaret Thatcher's heyday. After decades of being ignored and left behind, working-class voters seemed to be central to politics again. And this resurgence came not a moment too soon; working-class voters have continued to face the prospect of being economically marginalised, minimised in cultural life and abandoned educationally.

Sadly, for too many this new-found working-class voice is a source of regret rather than celebration. A new and insidious snobbery, aimed squarely at these voters, has taken root in part of elite society. For too many people, these election results didn't just mark a political disagreement, they also represented an unacceptable displacement of the natural order of things.

All of a sudden the 'wrong people', apparently uninformed and driven by bigotry, had proven decisive in electoral events. As a particularly angry editorial in *Foreign Policy* magazine put it, the divide was seen as 'between the sane and the mindlessly angry'.[1] To disagree with the status quo was to display a level of ignorance that shouldn't just be disagreed with but blatantly disregarded as 'insane' or based on mindless stupidity. This effortless superiority, writing off much of the country as barely worthy of being taken seriously, has become the calling card for much of contemporary progressive Britain.

Large parts of the often liberal, professional elite seem to believe that working-class views are not of the same worth as professional views; working-class jobs are not as valuable as middle-class jobs; and working-class places are less desirable to live in than middle-class places. This has created a new snobbery, through which it has become socially acceptable for the economically successful to look down on working people.

What actually constitutes working class is obviously a

discussion that has raged for centuries. For the purposes of this book, we'll largely define working class based on education (not in receipt of a degree) and occupation, although it is also worth noting that the majority of people still define themselves as working class, despite decades of commentary suggesting the opposite. The British Social Attitudes Survey indicates that 60 per cent of people regard themselves as working class, and notes that 'the proportion who consider themselves working class has not changed since 1983'.[2] Only around 35 per cent of the country had a degree when that was measured in 2012, but because of the expansion of higher education this figure could well be higher now.

TWO TIERS

For too much of elite Britain, a tone of disdain against the traditional working class represents the only socially acceptable form of prejudice. This is particularly, but not exclusively, on the liberal left, where the disdain is based sometimes on pity, sometimes on rage.

Words like ignorant and racist are thrown around freely and unfairly. Despite polling evidence that levels of racism in the UK are declining and are lower than in most of Europe, critics are keen to stereotype Brexit Britain as a dystopia of bigotry. The response to political changes driven by working-class voters isn't to accept that such alterations were based on considered choices and legitimate grievances but instead to insist that views that the managerial elite personally disagree with must be based on poor education, parochialism or a lack of sufficient enlightenment. For many politicians of the left, which is now a largely middle-class, city-based movement, the working-class vote now represents a reactionary obstacle to their progressive worldview.

Some Labour politicians in working-class areas have long regarded many of their constituents as some kind of embarrassing elderly relative, to be humoured come election time but otherwise largely ignored. As part of an explosive post-election argument, the former MP for Doncaster claimed that a Labour frontbencher and Islington MP told an MP from a Leave-voting constituency that she was 'glad my constituents aren't as stupid as yours'. Although Emily Thornberry has strongly denied making the comment, the fact that such stories are believable says much about the resurgence of snobbery. As former Home Secretary Alan Johnson reminded a leading Corbynista on election night: 'The working classes have always been a disappointment' for the left.[3] Another Labour MP, Dawn Butler, said, 'If anyone doesn't hate Brexit … then there is something wrong with you.'[4] The political decisions that have been galvanised by working-class towns have led commentators and politicians to lament a crisis of democracy, otherwise defined as democracy producing the wrong results.

Comedians, who are first to loudly claim to be offended in most circumstances, are the first to savage so-called 'crap towns' within the UK and ridicule narrow-minded, proletarian values. The likes of the BBC's *The Mash Report* and Radio 4's *The News Quiz* had a regular habit of punching down. Now popular theories allege that white working-class voters are the arch representatives of the newly popular concept of 'white privilege' or 'white fragility'. Working-class men are either caricatured as football hooligans or 'gammons'. Working-class patriotism is condemned and belittled, with book titles such as *52 Times Britain Was a Bellend* causing a stir amongst the anti-patriotic new snobs. Parts of the professional middle class have shown themselves unwilling or unable to treat many working-class views, attitudes and cultures with anything other than contempt. A left-wing radio DJ commented on a poll giving the Conservatives a lead in the Hartlepool by-election with the musing that the town's voters backing Tories was down to 'forelock-tugging stupidity', adding that the voters were 'thick as pigshit or pig ignorant'.[5]

Once the scale of the Hartlepool defeat for Labour had become clear, elements of the left indulged in another round of electorate blaming. One claimed that the problem for the left was that 'a huge number of the general public are racists and bigots' and asked, 'How do you begin to tackle entrenched idiocy like that?' Another claimed, 'We don't have an opposition problem. We have an electorate problem.' Hartlepool was yet more proof that the electorate don't take particularly kindly to being sneered at and being told repeatedly that they are wrong, stupid or both. Results like the Hartlepool by-election and Labour losing control of Durham Council, the first it had gained as a party in 2019, was further evidence that a realignment, accelerated by left-wing snobbery towards working people, was continuing apace.[6]

THE PERMANENT CITADELS OF THE NEW SNOBBERY

Whilst working-class voters have been making their voices heard at the ballot box for the first time in decades, the new snobbery has strengthened its hold over other important institutions in British life, including the judiciary, upper echelons of the media and government agencies. Despite an obsession with diversity, decision-making bodies in culture, business and broadcasting have little or no real representation of working-class life nor provincial towns. This results in decisions that often seem made in defiance of the majority of UK citizens. Activist judges and power-sucking quangos have gradually increased their power over the years. These bodies have become permanent institutions of minoritarian dominance, the embodiment of the managerial elite, very much separate from the democratic sphere and using their power to entrench norms and values anathema to many working-class voters.

Universities, despite conscious efforts to broaden their social bases, have remained resolutely middle class (only 13 per cent of white working-class boys on free school meals attend). Indeed, attending university has almost become an inherited right amongst the professional middle class, building up borders and boundaries between them and the so-called uneducated majority. Vocational education is routinely mentioned as 'a good idea' by politicians and commentators, but for the professional middle class it is only a good idea for other people's children.

Underpinning this new snobbery has been an all-embracing cult of meritocracy: the belief that success is always and everywhere down to hard work and talent, whilst lack of success is based on individual failure. Hence the snobbery of the successful towards the views of the less successful is seen as being justified by merit and talent. This has coincided with a two-tier economy created by the decline of skilled manufacturing and the growth of graduate jobs. Deindustrialisation created a social and economic blight that impacted several generations and is still being felt today. 'Wealth creators' have become lionised; professional careers have been defined as the only reasonable option; and superstar CEOs have grown used to seeing their views venerated in a cult-like way. At the other end of the social scale, many jobs have been robbed of dignity and respect and workers have found their voices ignored.

TILTED POLITICS AND ECONOMICS

For over three decades, politics, economics and culture became tilted in favour of the metropolitan middle class and the south-east and London. Politicians were predominantly from this professional background, and economic policies were predominantly designed to benefit these voters. This approach to economics saw a focus on delivering 'value' for shareholders and executives rather than investing in and respecting workers. Prosperity, success and growth tended to be pooled amongst the successful. Others saw decades of stagnation. The only possible goal for those 'left behind' was to aspire to join the professional middle class themselves. This tilting saw working-class voters robbed of economic power, political representation and cultural engagement.

The tidal wave of snobbery that accompanied the attempt to restore some economic dignity and political control was based on the overriding belief amongst much of the professional middle class that they had the right to have the game tilted in their favour. The snobbery didn't emerge with Brexit or the collapse of the Red Wall, but those events made such views seem acceptable and pushed them to the forefront of political discourse. And this denigration of the traditional working class came at a time when they needed political and economic backing more than ever. As mentioned above, these communities have been hit by decades of stagnation since the loss of industry, damaged by languishing real wages since 2008 and were amongst the hardest hit by the economic impacts of Covid. Political inequality has seen working-class voices marginalised, with some 85 per cent of MPs being graduates; economic inequality has seen hard work go unrewarded, with almost two decades of stagnating wages; educational inequality sees less intelligent rich children overtake poorer children by the age of six. White working-class boys – hardly a fashionable group to champion – have become the most educationally disadvantaged group in the country.

NEW SNOBS AND OLD SNOBS?

For a while, snobbery seemed to be restricted to a few cranks and eccentrics. The old school tie still mattered, and a handful of people still became agitated over whether 'loo' or 'toilet' was the right word to use. But the old concept that there was a link between social background and human worth seemed old fashioned half a century ago. People would have been incredibly reluctant to express this snobbery in public and would almost certainly have been castigated for it if they had.

The new snobbery is different from the old and is, in many ways, more harmful. It is much more likely than the old to doubt the ability of the poorer and less well educated to play a proper and informed role in a democracy. Indeed, in many ways modern snobbery has more in common with the anti-democratic oligarchs of the eighteenth and nineteenth centuries than the often ridiculed snobs of the post-war period. The old snobbery often went unspoken, whereas the new often dominates cultural output. A shared national experience, including the sacrifice of world wars, helped to erode class boundaries and bolster national solidarity, whereas the new snobbery is built from diminished national solidarity and limited shared experience. Today's snobbery seems worryingly acceptable and bites at the heart of modern Britain. A successful professional elite feels that they owe their position to talent rather than birth and feels comfortable making public their disregard for the views, habits and culture of the working class.

More and more, the elite not only live separately from the rest of society, with mixed communities a thing of the past, but have next to no social interaction whatsoever. Aside from a social and economic gap, too often the impression is given that a great swathe of metropolitan, professional Britain doesn't much like their fellow citizens and feels at best resentful of any economic and political influence they might have. The common patriotism that used to unite people is now often not felt by the metro-politan class. Social bonds and sympathies are limited, and institutions that once bound the classes together are no longer in existence. A snobbery at the top has often been responded to with resentment from those being looked down upon, as threads of solidarity have frayed. This gulf in understanding is not inevitable. It could be replaced with a pro-worker politics of the common good that aims to recapture a feeling of social solidarity and provides greater power and representation to working people.

TOWARDS A PRO-WORKER POLITICS

Our goal must be a politics that delivers power, accountability and opportunity to people long deprived of all three, helping to restore a sense of societal solidarity and the common good. This will mean moving beyond rhetoric and pushing forward an agenda that involves a genuine and lasting shift of power to working people. If the Conservative Party wants to make the temporary realignment of Labour voters in 2019 into a permanent one, only an agenda that genuinely enhances the strength, pride and esteem of working people will suffice. This will mean ending the disproportionate power of capital over labour; restoring the dignity of work and the strength of vocation and manufacturing; and giving working people a voice in the as yet impenetrable cultural bastions.

CHAPTER ONE

THE POLITICAL MARGINALISATION OF THE WORKING CLASS

'These fat old racists won't stop blaming the EU when their sh*t hits the fan … Absolute sh*tbag racist w*nkers.'
LABOUR MP, SEPTEMBER 2020[1]

'An ex-miner sitting in the pub calling migrants cockroaches … is not the [sort of] person we are interested in.'
PAUL MASON, 2019[2]

'The proletariat has discredited itself terribly.'
ENGELS TO MARX IN THE 1860S AS WORKING-CLASS VOTERS SUPPORTED 'REACTIONARY' PARTIES FOLLOWING THE EXTENSION OF SUFFRAGE.[3]

Early on EU referendum night in June 2016, the emphatic Leave vote in Sunderland made the political establishment aware that things were not going entirely to plan for the Remain campaign. Equally emphatic votes then followed in town after town, and it was clear that the working-class vote was driving a shuddering rebuke to the political, cultural and business elite. The entire establishment had lined up behind the Remain campaign as part of what David Cameron ensured voters was a 'once-in-a-lifetime decision'. The final poster of the Remain effort couldn't have been more emphatic: 'Leave', it promised, 'and there's no going back.'

Despite these fine words, once the Sunderland vote became clear, social media brimmed with righteous indignation and angry words. 'Ignorant idiots,' from places described as 'sh*tholes' and worse by angry Remain supporters, were condemned for 'stealing our future'. As dozens more towns like Sunderland, including my hometown of Consett, delivered equally resounding verdicts, the class hatred from parts of middle-class Twitter became more and more virulent. A viral petition the day after the vote, calling for the result to be overturned because of the folly of the masses, gained momentum, with another eventually gaining over 4 million signatures.

Snobbery was back. But the modern snob had dispensed with the monocle and waistcoat and was instead armed with a social media account, a mountain of self-righteousness and, in many cases, an angry opinion column. The belief that Brexit was the result of something between mass hysteria and mass stupidity allowed a lingering sense of suspicion about less-educated people to boil over into open snobbery. This new snobbery was more damaging than the old because it was deemed to be socially acceptable. The elite who had dominated the politics and economics of the previous decades were quick to denounce the ill-informed mob, with the same virulence that many of their predecessors in the eighteenth and nineteenth centuries had used to warn of the 'dangers of democracy'.

As the dust settled in the days and weeks after the referendum, many of the modern elitists made clear their view that this was an unacceptable overturning of the natural order of things. The British meritocracy had, they argued, ensured that the most talented were doing well in the new knowledge economy and the least talented, without the ambition or the get up and go to succeed, had been 'left behind' by their own lack of education and intelligence. The new snobs screamed repeatedly that these ignorant fellow citizens should not be able to crush their European dream.

Leave voters were quickly derided as low-information, low-intelligence people and were accused of being sold what John Major mocked as a 'fantasy'. The elite response was both hostile to the working class and, in some ways, virulently anti-northern. This backlash was marked by anger at the working class for ignoring the warnings of their perceived betters. We were repeatedly told that they were 'turkeys voting for Christmas' without the sufficient nous to understand that they were apparently voting against their own economic interests. At times, the snobbish backlash descended into outright nastiness, such as when Remainers said they hoped the Nissan plant in Sunderland would close because Sunderland's 'stupid Leave voters would deserve it'. Others said they would be 'pleased' if the fishing industry was harmed by Brexit as '*they* [my emphasis] got what they voted for'.

Few took a step back and considered why a political and business elite responsible for the Iraq War, the banking crash, and the biggest growth in insecurity and squeeze in living standards for almost two centuries should be meekly thanked by a grateful electorate for their superior wisdom. Instead, great swathes of the elite turned their anger on the voters who had dared to point out that the status quo wasn't working for them. They didn't consider that voters in the north, who had seen the economy go from industrially dominant to one of the least productive in Europe, might have had a point when they refused to celebrate south-eastern prosperity and the loss of investment and infrastructure in their areas. The fact that, according to the Institute for Fiscal Studies, the UK is one of the most geographically unequal economies in the OECD wasn't regarded as a justifiable reason to protest through the ballot box, following a referendum campaign that had celebrated what was described as decades of prosperity.

It wasn't considered logical that voters in the north-east, long ignored or taken for granted, had a legitimate griev- ance that their GDP per person had shrunk to less than half of that in London. The new snobs instead returned to pre-democratic language that questioned the ability of the mass of voters to make up their own minds.

The post-industrial working class might have been pivotal in two of our most recent major electoral events, but many of their political opponents could not hide their contempt in their reactions. A bulk of these residual Re- mainers had done very well out of the economic modern- isation that had left so many behind. Many professional circles in big cities simply assumed that their educated colleagues had voted Remain, and many couldn't hide their disdain for those from other parts of the country and in less successful parts of the economy. Few even stopped to acknowledge that this phase of political polar- isation was partially driven by an *economic* polarisation that decision-makers had long ignored.

OPEN SEASON FOR SNOBBERY

Open snobbery towards working-class voters has been on display since the 2016 referendum – a blatant lack of belief in the ability of lesser educated voters to make valid political decisions, combined with ugly, often contemp- tuous, language. This snobbery is accompanied by more systemic disengagement of the working classes. Despite the increased political importance of these voters, they remain badly unrepresented across politics and shut out from a variety of institutions.

The Labour Party, the traditional vehicle for working-class interests, is now, in the words of its own internal report, the party of 'high-status city dwellers'.[4] The political left has come to represent a credentialed and wealthy elite with what Christopher Lasch described as 'a satisfying sense of personal righteousness', who often see working people as reactionary barriers to progress.[5] The Conservatives have started to transform their voting coalition and now command greater working-class support than Labour. They have done so by backing away from market fundamentalism, but a large portion of the right-wing element of the political class remains in thrall to the economic liberalism that caused many of the issues we face today.

The political class continues to be dominated by high-status, professional graduates with the views and values generally representative of that group. Some combination of freedom of movement, freedom of capital, unfettered free trade and various elements of economic and social liberalism are common currency amongst them. Often vapid TED Talks are venerated, and counter-culture imagery is used to obscure the fact that priority is given to policies that benefit the professional class, such as open borders and the abolition of tuition fees, rather than policies that would benefit the wider population, such as building dignity at work or tackling the housing crisis.

Praiseworthy social progress, such as the legalisation of gay marriage, can't obscure the fact that the politics of the pre-referendum period had been almost predominantly run in the interests of the professional middle class, and that working people have continued to fall further behind. Although politicians have courted the working class with appeals to 'strivers' or 'alarm-clock Britain', governments of all parties have consistently promoted finance over manufacturing and graduates over non-graduates. In ten years, spending on higher education increased by 43 per cent, whilst spending on further education fell by up to 23 per cent.

Not only has politics has become less representative of working-class voters, with almost 90 per cent of MPs now being graduates, there is also a growing values gap between mainstream voters and the political class. As we will come to in more detail later in this chapter, the views of voters in general, tilting to the left economically and to the right culturally, remain badly underrepresented. That class remains highly devoted to social or economic liberalism (or both). Those members of the political class who understand the need to tackle economic insecurity are often devoted to a cultural liberalism, and those who understand cultural insecurity are often devoted to policies that accelerate economic insecurity.

The only possible route for British politics is one that backs away from snobbish attitudes and focuses on ensuring everybody, whether they have a university degree or not, is able to make a good, secure, dignified living, and one that allows working-class voices to again be represented at the heart of British life.

ALL OPINIONS ARE EQUAL, BUT SOME OPINIONS ARE MORE EQUAL THAN OTHERS

To paraphrase Orwell, too many people in modern Britain believe that 'all opinions are equal, but some opinions are more equal than others'. The traditional working class now see their views sneered at and frowned upon from across the political spectrum, but particularly on the modern left. Elites, long used to having their worldview accepted unquestioningly, have reacted to the renewed importance of working-class voters with barely hidden disdain. Political difference, apparently, isn't down to logical thought or first-hand experience but due to ignorance, racism and stupidity.

This has led to a democracy in which large parts of

the elite hold the views of the public in different levels of esteem, with the views of the traditional working class having less validity than the opinions of the professional middle class. Elements of the elite, happy to accept the misplaced view that economic success is down to talent rather than good fortune, have extended this concept to the belief that the professional middle class are the modern equivalent of philosopher kings – better able to make public policy decisions than their less educated and less economically fortunate countrymen.

Professional disdain for working-class views has created a grotesque inequality of political worth. This is multiplied by the existence of what some academics have described as educationalism or credentialism, with intolerance based on levels of educational achievement seen as the only acceptable type of prejudice. This is particularly injurious in the UK, where working-class young people are consistently let down by the education system. This then leads to a situation where the traditional working class are not only let down educationally but also marginalised economically and either ignored or mocked politically. One poll in the US even found that almost a fifth of American liberals would be upset if an immediate family member married somebody who hadn't been to university. It would be a surprise if such a result wasn't replicated in the UK.

A cross-university study in 2016 concluded that

> in contrast with popular views of the higher educated
> as tolerant and morally enlightened, we find that higher
> educated participants show education-based intergroup
> bias: they hold more negative attitudes towards less ed-
> ucated people than towards highly educated people ...
> Less educated people are seen as more responsible and
> blameworthy for their situation ... meritocracy beliefs are
> related to higher ratings of responsibility and blamewor-
> thiness, indicating that the processes we study are related
> to ideological beliefs.[6]

In other words, lack of education, which is increasingly
correlated to class, is now used by the better educated
to justify prejudice against poorer citizens. The research
also showed that many wealthier, better educated citizens
were unapologetic about feeling this disdain and happy to
blame the less successful for their own misfortune.

French sociologist Pierre Bourdieu went as far as condemning a bigotry of intellect. This allowed the creation
of what he called a 'theodicy of the elite', which justified
the social order and rationalised existing privileges. Such
a pattern can clearly be seen in the way the political
views of less educated citizens are all but written off by
many parts of the professional elite. A healthy democracy

cannot be one that sees a large part of the elite regarding the majority with contempt.

BIGOTS? HOW POLITICAL SNOBBERY BURST OUT INTO THE OPEN

Post-referendum research showed that professional (AB) voters were the only social group to have a considerable Remain sentiment, backing continued EU membership by around 18 per cent. For finance workers in the City of London, the gap was over 40 per cent.[7] By contrast, around two thirds of working-class voters and half of lower-middle-class voters opted to leave. In the post-referendum maelstrom, it was the voices of the professional class who were heard loudest across the media.

Working-class voters found their comparative lack of education weaponised against them. For the first time in decades, it became legitimate in many circles to regard the working class as undereducated and incapable of making complex political decisions. Snobbery went from being seen as a strange 1950s affliction of clipped accents and dated chatter reminiscent of Nancy Mitford's 'U and non-U', with its agitated discussion about napkins or serviettes attempting to differentiate U (upper-class) from non-U (non-upper-class) speech, to being almost a prerequisite for acceptance in parts of progressive Britain. This ranged from coded condescension to outright and unfiltered snobbery.

Prominent academics dredged up the prospect of 'mob rule' and argued there was a crisis of democracy (which seemed code for democracy producing the wrong results), with voters lacking sufficient education to make informed decisions. The rhetoric recalled the oligarchic arguments against suffrage extension in the nineteenth century. A leading centre-right columnist said it was clear that bigotry was the driving force behind the vote, whilst another described London's relationship to provincial towns as like 'being shackled to a corpse'.[8] The concept of an 'elite uprising' against the 'ignorant masses' was soberly discussed by a learned magazine, and one economist suggested restricting the franchise to those able to pass a 'minimum standards' intelligence test.[9]

Jason Brennan, an American academic, was bold enough in 2016 to make a case 'against democracy', arguing that democracy represents rule by the 'ignorant and the irrational' and should be replaced with a modern version of Plato's epistocracy or 'noocracy', where experts rule in an 'aristocracy of the wise'. Some protested that the problem in modern society is 'too much democracy' rather than economic insecurity. Others argued that voters need to be more aware of their own limitations and more grateful of the expertise of specialists and elites. One author wrote a book in defence of elitism. The likes of Brennan were bolder than most, but the message was a common one: democracy only works when it is guided by an elite and run in the best interests of that elite.

In the Brexit referendum, echoes of this refrain were to be found in the Remain campaign's complaint to the BBC that the Corporation's coverage would have 'a FTSE 100 CEO and then someone who makes a couple of prams in Sheffield'.[10] A prominent Leave supporter from County Durham, who left his fashion degree to help the Leave campaign, was regularly lambasted as 'just being a hair-dresser' and was the regular recipient of snobbish abuse on social media.

When the Remain campaign wasn't looking to blame foreign interference for their first defeat, they lamented the Leave voters who had 'voted against their own interests' (presumably because they had failed to comprehend those interests) or selfishly voted to 'steal our futures'. At no point were they prepared to acknowledge that working-class Leave voters cast their ballots for varied, rational and logical reasons, rather than being fuelled by hatred or ignorance.

SNOBBERY LEGITIMISED?

The *New European* became the house journal of the new snobbery that emerged from the EU referendum. Perhaps its clearest moment of class hatred came when it transformed Skegness's 'Jolly Fisherman' symbol into a vulgar caricature, flashing the V-sign and wearing a jumper that merely read 'Go Away'. According to the magazine, this caricature was 'so Brexit'.[11]

For great chunks of the Remain campaign, the ability for middle-class professionals to freely travel was more important than the impact of unlimited freedom of movement on the wages of those at the bottom. This emphasised how much of the Remain campaign was aimed squarely at the interests of middle-class professionals. The Erasmus university exchange scheme (which had only 14 per cent of participants from below average income backgrounds) was portrayed as a major issue, as were second homes on the continent. One prominent Remain campaigner, who suggested he wasn't aware of socio-economic inequality until after the referendum result, even used his spell in a French ski resort as an argument for EU membership. This wasn't restricted to the fringes of the Remain movement. Former Liberal Democrat leader and Business Secretary Vince Cable said that Leave voters were motivated by a desire for a world in which 'passports were blue, faces were white and the map was coloured imperial pink'.[12]

Later, the People's Vote campaign was based on an argument that the public should be given a chance to vote again on the issue because they weren't 'fully informed' the first time. The push for a rerun of the referendum was consistently characterised by a degree of elite disdain for ordinary voters. Those in working-class northern seats saw this call for a people's vote for what it was, leading to the dramatic collapse of Labour's once solid heartlands in December 2019.

Even years after the referendum, when the result was settled for most, one of the country's most politically active QCs (and Brexit had revealed an alarming number of politically active QCs with little political nous) made the peculiar suggestion that 'there was no agency in the Brexit vote. People voted on the basis of untruths … When you are scammed, you are scammed.'[13] It was seemingly only the highly educated people, such as QCs, who could see through this 'scam'.

In truth, this snobbery had long been just beneath the surface. There was, however, little reason for it to be articulated when a managerial elite saw their concerns being prioritised by politicians and decision-makers, as they had been over previous decades. The snobbery burst into the open when the referendum result threatened this comfortable status quo.

And this snobbery continues to dominate political debate, with increasingly offensive caricatures often taking the place of rational discussion. Over the course of a few weeks in mid-2020, a number of examples showed how pervasive it had become. Social media was alight with self-congratulation about a work of modern art that had appeared in Bristol. The sculpture was of an overweight man in a wheelie bin, wearing a string vest. The sculpture featured the words: 'Spoiler Alert: St George was Turkish.' It was a clear display of neo-snobbery, accompanied by the smug condescension that overflows from Twitter every St George's Day. Only a few days earlier, a media producer rightly criticised the behaviour of some far-right thugs in Parliament Square, only to also suggest that they looked like they had been 'born in a Wetherspoons'. The following week, social media was again ablaze with criticism of working-class people queuing in a perfectly socially distanced way outside Primark. One comment even suggested that we might cure Covid, but we'll never 'find a cure for people's stupidity'.[14] A Labour MP then launched a bizarre attack on 'fat old racists' following a row about the Last Night of the Proms.[15] It seems that fat-shaming is only acceptable when it comes in the guise of middle-class jibes at working-class people.

All of these examples indicate a divergence of values between the professional elite and working-class voters. They also indicate a divide in respect, with many looking down on their fellow citizens with barely disguised elite disdain.

LABOUR: 'THE SNOOTY PARTY'?

Many of the people who display some of the worst elements of elite disdain would recoil at being called snobs.

Some of the more interesting and perceptive voices on the left were amongst the first to point out that working people had been marginalised. But the end result of the left critique was to create a primarily metropolitan and middle-class movement that shifted the left even further from the values of working people.

Labour, the left would argue, is the party of the working class, so how can it be dominated by snobs? This is, sadly, a Labour Party that no longer exists. The party emerged from those great institutions of working-class life: the chapel and the trade union. To 'be Labour' used to be almost an extension of communal identity. No longer. The former coalfields voted for Brexit almost in their entirety, and it was these once solidly working-class communities that defied the prediction of the Labour Party chairman that 'the north just won't vote Tory'. Lord Glasman, the founder of Blue Labour, describes Labour as being 'out of relationship with its history, traditions and the communities that created and cherished it. So out of touch that it couldn't see the rejection coming.'[16] A Labour Party that was once given meaning by industrial communities had turned its back on the values of the people living in these communities. In turn, these voters noticed the rejection and returned the favour.

The Labour governments of Ramsay MacDonald and Clement Attlee (particularly the former) lived up to the party's roots and were dominated by manual workers and non-conformists. Today's Labour Party is very different. The proportion of Labour MPs who were manual workers has fallen from almost 20 per cent in 1979 to less than 3 per cent today. Labour MPs are now overwhelmingly white-collar professionals and university educated (over 80 per cent – more than the Conservatives). This change has very much been noticed by people living in working-class towns. As Deborah Mattinson, pollster and author of the excellent *Beyond the Red Wall*, concluded: 'Once the party of the working class, it [Labour] was now the "snooty" party, peopled by posh southern graduates who looked down on the Red Wall and the things they cared most about.'[17] As the Labour Together report into the 2019 election summarised, this led to Labour being 'rejected by many of the communities [it was] founded to represent.'[18]

By 2021, Labour had become an overwhelmingly middle-class, professional, metropolitan party with values and priorities that reflected this background. Research by Queen Mary University of London found that almost 80 per cent of Labour members are middle class. And YouGov polling shows quite how far the party membership has become detached from those communities in which it was founded. The study found that only a quarter of Labour members believed in *any* immigration controls whatsoever; only 15 per cent said they were proud of British history, whereas almost half said they were ashamed;

only a fifth said they would be happy or proud to sing the national anthem; and more blamed the British government than the IRA for the Troubles in Northern Ireland. These viewpoints are all anathema to the working-class communities that remain patriotic, in favour of sensible immigration restrictions and which often saw their sons and grandsons join the military and serve in Northern Ireland – and were proud of that service.

This transformation of the British left from a working-class patriotic tradition to a middle-class Universalist* tradition is part of what Thomas Piketty has described as the Brahminisation of Social Democratic parties. He argues that both left- and right-wing traditions have been captured by middle-class elites, creating a Brahmin Left and a Merchant Right, with working-class voices left out. For Piketty, parties of the centre-left changed their priorities, meaning that improving the lot of the disadvantaged stopped being their main focus, and these concerns were replaced with those of the highly educated, aspirational voters.

American commentators such as Michael Lind and Thomas Frank have also pointed to that country's left becoming an increasingly professional elite project.

---

* A belief that ideas have universal applicability. This is in contrast to the idea that Labour gained much of its ideas and vibrancy from the communities in which it was founded. Traditionally, as Harold Wilson famously said, Labour owed more to the ideas expressed in the Methodist chapels that were once omnipresent in mining villages than it did to the universalism of Karl Marx.

Frank's description of the US Democrats as reflecting 'in virtually every detail, the ideological idiosyncrasies of the professional-managerial class'[19] could just as easily apply to the Labour Party. It is in the UK, however, where the transformation has been most complete, with a generation seeing some communities transform from being culturally firmly Labour to having their cultural politics defined by a Conservative Brexit.

Elements of the British left have tried to embrace a new form of metropolitan identity politics which prioritises issues such as race and gender. In doing so, the concerns of the traditional working class have been relegated to the bottom of a list of identity-driven priorities. For much of the left, working-class voters represent a reactionary barrier to the achievement of their goals. In many ways, this represents a continuation of the New Left tradition of the 1960s, which regarded students, rather than the working classes, as the drivers of progress. This movement led Richard Hofstadter to criticise an elitism based on 'moral indignation against most of the rest of us'.[20] That spirit is alive and well in the British left today. The modern left has carried on the New Left's view that patriotism, borders and traditional institutions are somehow backward – placing a substantial barrier between them and the patriotic working class.

At the same time, elements of the modern left have found it hard to let go of some of the old rhetoric of class.

Condemning 'toffs' and championing the broad mass of 'workers' often goes hand in hand with denouncing some of those workers for holding 'backward' views.

Many still talk about the working class in a romantic way, and plenty attend the Durham Miners' Gala on an annual basis, as though they're attending a Disneyland of their romanticised working class. At the same time, the growth of hobbyist leftism has led to the bizarre situation in which some left-wing flag wavers claim to champion the working class at the same time as denouncing them in front of audiences of radicalised middle-class professionals. Commentator Paul Mason, for example, indulged in crude caricature about retired coal miners holding reactionary opinions and went on to argue that the modern left should not be interested in the votes of that 'sort of person'. They should, he suggested, seek the votes of so-called progressives instead. Following the election, he was keen to argue that 'at no point did Labour "desert" the working class'. Instead, the working class had deserted Labour and 'I am not going to flinch from stating that in the places it did so there is now a toxic narrative of nativism and xenophobia.'[21] Blaming the voters for an election defeat isn't new on the left, but, to paraphrase Mason, it's so much worse when combined with a toxic mix of snobbery and condescension.

Another prominent left-wing commentator chose the week before the collapse of the Red Wall to dispute the idea that Labour had lost the working class and engage in intellectual contortions, such as redefining the working class so middle-class students were included. Such ideas bring to mind the ironic suggestion by Bertolt Brecht after the 1953 East German uprising, that it would be easier for the government 'to dissolve the people and elect another'. Labour's attitude towards the contemporary working class is all too reminiscent of when Engels complained to Marx in 1868 that the working class had 'discredited itself terribly' by embracing reactionary views.[22]

Old tropes are regularly rolled out, such as false consciousness and the working class being duped by a right-wing media – a cliché that underlines the lack of faith of many on the left that working-class people can make the right decision without the guidance of middle-class progressives. On so many issues – national security, welfare, patriotism, Brexit – the people who once stood for the organised working class now seem ranged against them. This divide isn't just one of organisation; it is also fundamentally one of values, with representatives of the elite standing for a social and, at times, economic liberalism, whilst working people stand for more communitarian values.

What is clear, however, is that despite a shift under the leadership of Keir Starmer, many of the values, traditions and concerns of working-class voters are now alien to many Labour MPs and members. The phrase 'the snooty party' touches a nerve because it is so close to the truth, and it will take more than a change at the top of the party to alter that values-driven perception.

THE RETREAT OF TRADE UNIONS

Trade unions have a fundamental role to play in tackling the economic marginalisation of working people. There is clearly a role for unions at a time when capital has disproportionate power over labour and the dignity of work needs to be revived. But trade unions in the UK have been in retreat for decades, shedding members and indulging in ideological hobby horses. They are failing to meet their obligations to workers, who feel that unions are alienating, outmoded or simply 'not for them'. This has meant that much of the traditional working class have little or no representation in the workplace at a time when they have seldom needed it more.

This is a far cry from the golden age of trade unions led by remarkable individuals such as Ernie Bevin, who helped increase the living standards of working people whilst showing that trade unions could be responsible industrial partners. Unions were one of a number of institutions, including churches and community organisations, that helped support the growth of the working-class voice and the improvement in wages and conditions. The founding focus of the Trades Union Congress (TUC) in

1868 seems oddly reminiscent of today's societal issues, with the priorities of the first congress being wage inequalities, workers' rights and the need to improve technical education.

The influence of unions over the formation of the Labour Party meant that union-affiliated MPs came from the shop floor and gave a real working-class voice to the corridors of power – what David Marquand described as 'labourism'. Indeed, what Martin Pugh termed 'Tory Socialism' – emphatic about improving pay and conditions for workers but also emphatically patriotic and robust – partially came from the influence of trade-union MPs. Ideological over-reach by the unions and lunatic industrial militancy meant that this voice was lost. Decades later, unions have never been weaker, and Labour MPs who represent union seats are as likely to be white-collar union researchers or public sector middle management.

Unions should be central to tackling the numerous maladies affecting working people today. Instead, they seem consumed by fringe elements and far-left thinking that does little to benefit their members. For example, major trade unions are weirdly obsessed with showing 'solidarity' with countries such as Venezuela and Cuba, both of which have diabolical human rights records and an indifferent approach to independent trade unions. Indeed, Cuba has no independent trade unions at all.

Yet over twenty trade unions are affiliated to the Venez-
uelan solidarity committee and their Cuban equivalent.
The RMT affiliates with the World Federation of Trade
Unions, which includes the North Korean union as a
prominent member. It is unclear what benefits this brings
to British workers and trade union members or why their
subs are being used by apologists for human rights abuses
and the curtailing of personal freedoms.

This is the most flagrant example of a trade union
movement that has become detached from its core purpose. In so doing, trade unions make themselves seem
irrelevant and extreme to millions of workers. Whereas
trade unions once represented the 'conservative' instincts
of the British working class (often coming from local political cultures and being robustly patriotic, anti-pacifist,
anti-temperance but resolutely in favour of better wages,
living standards and working conditions), their leadership
played a key role in pushing Labour leftwards in recent
years. Union political statements have veered wildly away
from protecting their members' interests. Major trade
unions have, for example, supported the Boycott, Divest-
ment, Sanctions campaign to boycott Israeli goods, and
union money has been wasted on court cases defending
hard-left websites against former Labour MPs. Little
wonder that a group of rank-and-file trade unionists have
condemned their union leadership for 'an obsession to

run the Labour Party – rather than represent the millions of workers who pay their subs into [the Unite general secretary's] union's bank account.[23]

This leftward shift has put trade union leadership at odds with the views of existing members, never mind the views of potential members. Almost 40 per cent of Unite members voted Conservative at the 2019 general election despite Unite being an architect of Jeremy Corbyn's left-wing political strategy. Only 12 per cent of the union's members even voted in the last election for general secretary, illustrating how disengaged union members have become from the politics of its leadership.

This deviation between union leaders and far-left activists is by no means a new thing. In 1979, for example, more trade unionists voted for Thatcher's Tories than Callaghan's Labour, partially in response to the capture of union leadership by parts of the hard left. Research by Lord Ashcroft in 2013 has even shown that most Unite members were deeply disengaged by the politics of the union's leadership. A majority opposed union policy on abolishing the Right to Buy, reducing the voting age to sixteen and contesting the introduction of a benefit cap (some 86 per cent supported this policy).

The obsession with fringe left issues that do nothing to improve conditions for workers and everything to alienate present and potential members has proved hugely counterproductive to both trade unions and the economy as a whole. In 1979, trade unions had a membership of over 13 million; that's now little more than 6 million. There are also a million more trade unionists in the public sector than in the private sector, with many of the lowest-paid parts of the private sector having no worker organisation at all. Just as working people need representation and organised labour more than ever, much of the trade union movement has fallen asleep at the wheel, seeming extreme and irrelevant to millions of workers.

The economy and millions of workers need the organisational support of a sensible trade union movement. Politics is also missing the fact that trade unions once represented an important source of MPs with lived experience of working-class life and an important link to working people. It is about time unions recommitted themselves to providing organisation and representation to workers, rather than becoming a mouthpiece for far-left views.

THE VALUES GAP

As we have seen, there is a clear and growing divide between Labour's membership and MPs and their traditional working-class base. This is one of many reasons why working-class voters, feeling that they lacked representation and an adequate voice, chose a referendum to ensure that their voice was heard, and the following election to ensure that this voice was not ignored. However, something that has seen less analysis is the more general divide between the values of the political class and the values of voters more generally.

Politicians have become more representative of parts of the population in recent years – rapidly when it comes to sexuality (at forty-five the UK now has more LGBT representatives than any other Parliament worldwide, and twenty of them are Conservatives) and gender (220 female MPs, compared to forty-one in 1987); and slowly with regard to ethnicity (sixty-five BAME MPs, compared to four in 1987). This progress hasn't been replicated regarding class. Some 44 per cent of Tory MPs went to fee-paying schools, with the new Tory intake – gushingly described as a 'flood of working-class Tories'[24] – still far surpassing the 7 per cent of the population who attend private schools. As we've already noted, the proportion of university-educated MPs has also dramatically increased in recent years, just as the proportion of manual workers who become MPs has fallen from around a fifth in 1979 to less than 3 per cent now. The values that MPs bring will much more likely be those of the minority of the country who attended university than the majority of the population who didn't.

Just as economists tell us that we are in a 'post-industrial' economy (Germany and Korea wisely ignored the memo), it seems that we have partially retreated to a pre-industrial model of politics, with the Commons representing the different concerns of the educated middle class. Industrialisation led to the formation of the Labour Party for those frustrated at the Liberal failure to elect working-class MPs and 'reflect working-class concerns', and for those dedicated to 'a distinct Labour group … engaged in promoting legislation in the direct interests of labour'.[25] As previously discussed, this led to decades of increased working-class representation in the Commons.* Post-industrialisation has, however, meant that the part of the population which don't have degrees and don't work in professional jobs are again badly unrepresented. Just like in the pre-industrial age, many middle-class 'progressives' now see it as their role to 'represent working-class interests', often with a tin ear to many of these concerns.

Some argue that it's a good thing that our representatives are now more educated. Sadly, this hasn't fed through into better governance and has instead merely created a crisis of representation and growing disengagement between the political elite and the rest of society. A Commons that had a majority of non-graduates was able to build the welfare state; the NHS; a public house-building programme that put today's efforts to shame; an economy that maintained skilled work and combined low inflation with low unemployment. The increase of graduates in the

---

* Keir Hardie's response when asked whether he was arriving in Parliament to work on the roof that he was actually there to 'work on the floor' may be apocryphal, but it is a strong symbol of the change in mentality that more working-class representation brought.

Commons has coincided with disasters such as the Exchange Rate Mechanism debacle; financial deregulation; the Iraq War; the banking crash; and the Great Recession.

The detached worldview held by many representatives, which arguably led to this menu of poor public policy, is often shared by party members, who are also disproportionately middle class. This is very much the case in the modern Labour Party but is also the case for the Conservatives and the Liberal Democrats. As a rule, Labour members and MPs are much more socially liberal than their voters and Conservative members and MPs are much more economically liberal than their voters. The same very much applies for many in what can be defined as the 'political class' of advisers, think tankers and union officials. They are much more likely to be middle-class graduates and more liberal than the rest of the population. Working in politics isn't always particularly well-paid, and people generally need the ideological inclination and financial wherewithal to work in politics in central London. Adviser Nick Timothy's tale about how he was encouraged to read Ayn Rand's ultra-libertarian tract *Atlas Shrugged* when he first started working at Conservative Central Office is deeply symbolic of the political class often being dogmatic about liberal ideologies that aren't shared by the majority of voters.

All of these factors mean that a disconnect can grow between the political class and most voters, and a 'groupthink' develops about how voters think and what the preferences and priorities should be. This was highlighted most notably by how many MPs in working-class constituencies expressed 'surprise' at the EU referendum result and the number who failed to understand the depth of feeling and resentment over proposals for a second referendum. It can also be seen in the near consensus of commentators who said that the gap in politics was for a socially liberal, economically liberal, pro-European party before Change UK fell flat on its face and the Liberal Democrats went backwards in 2019.

The disengagement of working-class voters can be clearly seen in the turnout figures in elections. In 1992, Ipsos MORI estimated that almost 80 per cent of working-class voters voted in that year's election. By 2015, turnout amongst this group was just over half. At the same time, the turnout 'gap' between working-class people and professionals became a gaping chasm, growing from a 6 per cent difference in 1992 to almost 20 per cent two decades later. At the 2019 election, the lowest-turnout constituencies were almost all predominantly working class (one in Hull couldn't even muster a turnout of more than half). It was only with the Brexit referendum, when working-class voters were able to protest at their values being ignored, that turnout ticked up. At the election in 2019, some working-class voters returned to their non-voting habit after seeing the political class use every procedural trick to prevent Brexit from happening. Others decided to use the same election to send an even more emphatic message to the political class not to ignore the message they had sent in 2016.

The continuing disconnect was highlighted by research by Tim Bale, Phil Cowley et al. at Queen Mary University. It showed that on a range of social issues, including respect for traditional values and tougher sentences for criminals, the British public is considerably more socially conservative than both Labour and Tory MPs. The public are also much more economically interventionist than most of the political class. Indeed, Conservative voters are way to the left economically of Conservative MPs, and this creates a key dilemma, which we will discuss later.

The fundamental division at the heart of British politics is illustrated by the contrast in economic and social values between voters and Conservative and Labour MPs, councillors, candidates and members. *All* of the major groups of voters are in the left wing economically but also relatively socially conservative quadrant – and particularly working-class voters. None of the political class can be found in that corner, with Conservatives clustered as economically liberal and socially conservative (with MPs more right-wing economically and more socially liberal) and Labour members of the political class clustered in the socially liberal and economic left. The political class still represents a type of politics in which most voters do not fully believe, much less identify with. The real common ground is where most working people sit – tilting slightly to the left economically and slightly more conservative culturally – and this worldview is one of the least likely to be represented amongst the political class. The fact that this worldview was unrepresented for so long led to the explosion of anger of the Brexit referendum, and if such ideas become unrepresented again, another outburst of disengagement and anger would surely be the most likely outcome. If anything, the 2016 referendum and elements of the 2019 election showed the electoral potency of a combination of economic interventionism and cultural conservatism. But most members of the political elite remain ideologically distant from the bulk of the people. The political class remains divorced from mainstream views in the country and deluded about what these views actually are.

This detachment is increased by the nature of the political media in the UK. Political columnists are generally middle class and cluster in the same political areas as Tory or Labour MPs. The values gap between the public and the elite means that extremes of right and left are more likely to be heard than the mainstream views of most Britons. Additionally, the desire for 'balance through confrontation' on behalf of the broadcast media also means that the far left and the libertarian right are over-represented. There are very few representatives of the politics of the majority who are relatively culturally conservative and economically interventionist. This means that broadcasters seek a fake 'balance' by ensuring that the 'left' and 'right' are adequately represented, whilst the common ground of the actual mainstream is nowhere to be seen.

UNTOUCHED BY DEMOCRACY? MINORI-TARIAN CITADELS OF ELITE DOMINANCE

Just as voters have shrugged off their deference to elite wisdom when they make decisions via the ballot box, some organisations have doggedly maintained the political power of the elite. They have become minoritarian institutions, often defending the worldview of an elite minority, untouched by the ballot box and full of the professional establishment, with views and backgrounds far removed from most voters. As the voices of voters have become louder so have the powers of the judiciary and various 'arm's-length' bodies, both, in their own ways, elitist and unaccountable.

The growth of judicial activism, which we once thought of as a curiously American affair, means that unelected and unaccountable pockets of elite power are growing stronger than ever. It has also created a fundamental transformation of the British constitution. Traditionally, via our Common Law system, power has resided in the people through Parliament and a system that encouraged political accountability and democratic debate. Under this system, the power of the judiciary in legislation has always been limited – judges don't review legislation; they merely act when governments are seen as acting illegally. This has changed fundamentally in recent years, with judges' power bolstered and Parliament's power diluted by EU membership, the introduction of the Human Rights Act and a sharp uptick in judicial review, with the judiciary playing a much more active role not just in reviewing legislation but also in effectively making and interpreting policy.

Judicial power continued to grow following the creation of the very un-British institution of the Supreme Court in 2009. Such judicial review effectively allows judges to override the democratic process and shifts power to a deeply socially exclusive, unaccountable group. Even the then Master of the Rolls was forced to admit that 'in the past few decades there has been a massive increase in the number of applications for judicial review'[26] and that such decisions 'inevitably involve making political judgments'.[27] Furthermore, Lord Sumption, former judge at the Supreme Court, has correctly argued that the growth in judicial power has continued to undermine both the legislative process and democratic accountability, with controversial issues, such as prisoners' voting rights, sentencing policy and euthanasia, becoming matters for the courts rather than in their rightful place: being vigorously debated in the democratic arena.

This growth in judicial power as a vestige of minoritarian dominance is underlined by the fact that elements of the judiciary are more out of touch in terms of social background than almost any other profession. Almost two thirds of judges attended fee-paying schools, 71 per cent went to Oxbridge and over half went to both private school and Oxbridge. The Sutton Trust commented: 'Senior judges are the most rarefied group ... far removed from even many fellow members of the elite.'[28] For decades, the left in British politics understood this, with figures such as legal scholar J. A. G. Griffith arguing that the narrow background of the judiciary means they cannot act in a neutral way but can only act politically in a way that preserves the power of elites. The infamous Taff Vale legal judgment in the early twentieth century, which made unions liable for the loss of profit to employers caused by strike action, stood as testament to this pro-elite bias for many years.

The growth in political power of the judiciary has been accompanied by a desire from both right and left to move this power away from Parliament and towards judges. The ability of 'well-informed' members of the judiciary to make policy via various legal mechanisms is seen as being much 'safer' than the alternative – policy-making through contested politics in a Parliament that represents the country as a whole. As legal philosopher Jeffrey Goldsworthy argued, part of this shift has been driven by the fact that a

> substantial proportion of the professional class has lost faith in the ability of their fellow citizens to form opinions about public policy in a sufficiently intelligent, well-informed, dispassionate and carefully reasoned manner. They may be attracted to judicial enforcement partly because it shifts power to people (judges) who are representative members of their own class, and whose educational attainments, intelligence, habits of thought, and professional ethos are thought more likely to produce enlightened decisions.[29]

In other words, the power of the judiciary has become another part of the political element of the new snobbery – professional power, backgrounds and views are effectively insulated from the pressures of what professionals have come to regard as the 'democratic mob'. Former Law Society president David Greene boasted that his legal practice 'has allowed me to pursue politics through the courts'.[30] The pursuit of politics shouldn't be insulated in this way from voters, as is the case with much judicial and public body power.

Public bodies, or arm's-length bodies, previously known

as quangos (quasi-autonomous non-governmental organisations), also remain an element of the body politic
insulated from democratic pressure and accountability. A
2015 report from a House of Commons select committee
described these public bodies as resembling a scene from
The Matrix, 'where doors open on virtual worlds which
are insulated from reality and hidden from the public and
from those meant to be accountable for them'.[31] They are
a crucial part of public policy-making and they continue
to be dominated by representatives of an elite consensus.
Each year, over 1,000 appointments are made to over 500
public bodies, which have multi-billion-pound budgets
and are hugely influential in developing public policy, as
well as in helping to implement this policy. Their boards,
which often play an important role in policy setting, are
entirely appointed by the government, with no oversight
from the public. As such, they remain immune from
many of the pressures faced by elected politicians and
from the pressure of public opinion.

Evidence suggests that in addition to being
unaccountable to the public, these bodies are also not
particularly representative of the public either. In 2018/19,
almost a third of appointments to public bodies lived in
London or the south-east. In comparison, only 2 per cent
were from the north-east of England. Whilst these public
bodies are by no means homogenous or monolithic, their
boards are much more likely to represent the professional

elite than working-class voters in the towns. A 2013 report on reforming public appointments by Pinto-Duschinsky and Middleton found that 'contemporary public life is dominated nearly exclusively by those from "higher managerial" occupations, with those in "intermediate" and "routine and manual" occupations barely represented at all'.[32] Almost half of the chairs of these bodies attended independent schools, and those responsible for selecting members of the agencies are almost entirely from upper-managerial occupations. The report also found that the number of women and ethnic minorities still needs to increase to represent the broader population, but it is people from working-class backgrounds who are most dramatically unrepresented. A 40 per cent increase of the number of women on public bodies and a 150 per cent increase in ethnic minority appointees would see public bodies achieve parity with their representation in the general population. The number of appointees from working-class backgrounds would need to increase by almost 900 per cent. Although the report was written in 2013, there is little sign of a substantial uptick since then.

Appointees within this professional elite are also relatively unlikely to be ideologically representative. For much of the past decade, despite the Conservatives being in government, appointments to boards still have Conservative supporters in the minority. In 2018/19, almost half of the public appointments who were politically active were

Labour supporters, and less than a third were Conservatives. This is not to diminish the importance of a wide variety of organisational or managerial skills. It remains important, though, that these bodies represent a much greater diversity of regional and social backgrounds. Otherwise, the bodies risk becoming bureaucratic symbols of minoritarian dominance, permanently in power regardless of election results. They also risk becoming self-perpetuating, recruiting from a limited social pool and looking to recruit others in their own image. They represent forms of permanent minoritarian governance that could stand in the way of democratic decisions.

CONSERVATIVES AT THE CROSSROADS

There has always been a deeply ingrained conservatism in many parts of working-class Britain, going all the way back to what Disraeli famously called 'angels in marble'. Love of place has always been fundamental to these towns – from love of the local community to a deep patriotism and passion for country. They have always been ingrained with a strong sense that work is about so much more than a pay cheque: that it provides dignity, security and a sense of worth. The fact that so many of these towns were defined by their industry is no accident. Family has always mattered, as has respecting what your ancestors did and built – it is 'ancestor worship', what Nye Bevan described as 'that most conservative of all religions'.

The conservatism that was on display in working-class communities was seldom of the sort that the national Conservative Party displayed. An association with deindustrialisation meant that the party seemed disinterested in dignity of work or strong communities. The shedding of many elements of conservatism in favour of an increasingly one-dimensional economic liberalism as the 1980s and '90s wore on didn't sit well with these communities either, especially when it was combined with a message that to be 'mobile' and 'successful' was to escape these communities. Post-2005 'Tory modernisation' was squarely aimed at the metropolitan middle class, with a short-lived cocktail of Thatcherite economics and social liberalism that didn't seem especially conservative.

This all began to change rapidly with the Brexit vote. The shift of the Labour Party to being the party of middle-class political hobbyists made the swing possible, but the Tory Party also had to change to make it happen. The move that started under Theresa May and then crystallised under Boris Johnson saw a shift away from myopic economic liberalism and accepted that the state had a role to play in the economy. This was reflected in a policy agenda that focused on using the state to 'level up' and the use of levers such as state aid.

This didn't go unnoticed and led to many towns that have been Labour for the best part of a century voting Tory – something that would have been unthinkable even a decade ago. Such a change is, of course, welcome and something that I've pressed for over a number of years, including in my 2019 book *Little Platoons*. This should, however, only be the beginning of the process. Working-class voters have, after all, heard grand promises before, and this hasn't always been matched by grand results.

A lasting change can only happen if working-class voters become central to everything the party says and does, ensuring that Conservative instincts and policies match more closely with those of their new electoral co-alition. There are thirty-three seats that the Conservatives could win with a swing of 4 per cent, and the majority of these are Red Wall-type seats with similar demographics to those won in 2019. An offer of economic and cultural security combined with a record of delivery in new Tory seats could also tilt these seats into the Tory column. Although the Tory Party has made great strides towards a way of thinking that eschews dogmatic small-statism in favour of a programme of ambitious transformation, there is still more to do in order to make the party permanently allied to the views of the mainstream majority of economically pragmatic and culturally conservative voters.

Ideologically, the bulk of the Tory Party continues to

be some distance from the views of mainstream voters, still more inclined to look to Hayek than Huddersfield for inspiration about policy. As we set out earlier, the political class remains distant from working-class voters, and in many cases that is as much the case with the attachment of some Tories to economic liberalism as it is with the close attachment of the left to identity liberalism. And there remain forces within the party that push against such a necessary adjustment to reflect the views and interests of voters.

Some on the libertarian right of the party remain convinced that the vote for economic reform in 2016 was actually a vote for dramatic cuts in regulation and an ultra-free trade, deregulatory small-state agenda. Any push ahead with such an agenda, popular amongst elements of the Tory Party in Westminster but not at all in the country, would risk alienating those new Tory voters who above all else want economic security, cultural continuity and political control.

Other dissenters from the Red Wall path are on the 'Cameron' wing of the party. Former Tory Cabinet members have even expressed a concern that their party's new dependence on working-class voters in the Red Wall could see their party shift away from a liberal approach to economics – without stopping to consider why these voters might be hesitant in their enthusiasm for such liberalism. One even lamented that the Tory

Party was 'lost for small-state free marketeers' because
of a dependence on the economic views of working-class
voters who, he argued, 'will cause economic problems'
and who have social views that would look 'divisive
and mean-spirited' in a way that will 'contaminate the
brand'.[33] Such a view is, thankfully, far less widely shared
in Tory circles than would have been the case a few years
ago. However, it represents a right-wing side of the new
snobbery that maintains a small-state dogmatism that
fails to see genuine economic problems and caricatures
people's desire for social continuity as one of bigotry.

Conservatives are now representing towns, from
Consett to Leigh, from Grimsby to Blyth, that once
seemed impenetrable Labour bastions. In order to bring
about lasting change, they must ensure that these towns,
their voters and their political priorities are represented at
every level within the Conservative Party, just as much as
they are by the newly elected Conservative MPs. In other
words, the 'political class' element of the Tory Party within
Whitehall and party HQ should represent working-class
views and interests. Efforts should continue to be made
to remove the Tory's 'party of the rich' reputation and
ensure that the pubs of Leigh and Blyth are as important
and as influential to the party as the black-tie events held
on Park Lane.

There will be times when the interests of working-class
voters come into conflict with vested interests in the

financial sector, and a Tory Party keen to sustain a new electoral coalition should always choose the former over the latter. It will be necessary for Conservatives to take decisions that might not always be beneficial to party donors. A one-eyed belief in the private sector right or wrong, including the dubious benefits of outsourcing and financialisation, might well run contrary to the interests of working people and their families. Instead, the party should accelerate the reorienting of its philosophy around dignified jobs, stronger industry and a shift of power to working people.

BUILDING A PRO-WORKER POLITICS

Since 2016, large parts of the political debate have been focused on working-class voters. Those who were firstly defined as the 'left-behind' voters who drove the Brexit vote and then the Red Wall voters who, in shifting historic loyalties, delivered the largest Tory majority for over thirty years. As we have seen, this movement of working-class concerns to be a central focus of politics hasn't been universally welcomed. Working-class priorities have been greeted with condescension by some elements of the liberal establishment. The Labour Party, the traditional representatives of these voters, has shifted its base to high-income city dwellers and the trade unions, the traditional organisational support for the working class, have also declined beyond all recognition. Parts of the modern left have made clear they don't much like elements of working-class Britain and are uninterested in winning their votes back.

Whilst the wider political class has signalled a need to listen to the views of working-class voters more, they remain ideologically much more liberal than the majority of voters. Although working-class votes are in the spotlight, the party machines and the political class that is pursuing these votes remains resolutely middle class. This means that, despite superficial progress, the working class are hit by a triple political whammy of rising snobbery from liberals; the side effects of 'woke politics' that serves to diminish their concerns; and a continued lack of representation amongst large sections of the political class, quangocracy and political media. This gap, ready to be filled, was highlighted in both 2016 and 2019. The future actions of both major parties will decide whether the 2019 election marked the beginnings of a politics in which the majority of people feel involved and engaged in the democratic process or a temporary deviation in liberal elite politics. If long-promised change doesn't arrive, then this is likely to provoke real anger in working Britain.

EXCLUDED: THE CULTURAL AND EDUCATIONAL ROOTS OF THE NEW SNOBBERY

'An elite, if it is a governing elite, so far as the natural impulse to pass on to one's offspring both power and prestige is not artificially checked, will tend to establish itself as a class.'

T. S. ELIOT[1]

'Why am I the first Kinnock in a thousand generations to be able to get to university? Was it because all our predecessors were "thick"? Did they lack talent? Was it because they were weak? Of course not. It was because there was no platform upon which they could stand.'

NEIL KINNOCK[2]

Disdain towards the lesser educated might have surged recently, but Jim Callaghan faced something close to the same wrath shortly after becoming Prime Minister in 1976, when he gave a speech to a room of 'educationalists'.

This avuncular and underrated Prime Minister, who left school at sixteen and worked his way up through the trade union movement, did something that was considered unthinkable for a Labour Prime Minister: he expressed his grave misgivings at various elements of the education system. There were mutterings beforehand about the impertinence of a man with little formal education lecturing such esteemed experts in the field; these mutterings became howls of disapproval once the speech had been delivered.

The speech was devoted to tackling some of the shibboleths beloved of the educational community. Callaghan made clear his belief that the goal of education was 'to equip children to the best of their ability for a lively, constructive place in society, and also to fit them to do a job of work. Not one or the other but both.'[3] He listed numerous reasons, from 'informal' learning methods through to a badly designed curriculum and examination system, to explain why state education was failing to do this. And the chief sufferers from this state of affairs were young people from working-class backgrounds.

As is often the case with a prophet in their own land, the points made by Callaghan were largely ignored at the time of his speech. However, it laid the groundwork for the debate that would dominate education for decades to come. Politicians as different as Tony Blair and Michael Gove pursued the cause of educational reform with impressive zeal, and important progress has been made, despite criticism from an educational establishment that disliked curriculum reform and shifting power to schools. Sadly, four and a half decades after Callaghan first warned of the issues, educational inequality remains stark, and the divides created by this disparity represent an important part in creating and entrenching snobbish divides.

From a young age, working-class children are let down by the education system. This is a pernicious and vicious cycle, since elements of the new snobbery are fuelled by what Michael Sandel called 'credentialism' – prejudice by the highly educated towards the lesser educated. A tendency towards 'elite production', where the already successful live in the same communities as other well-educated people, marry well-educated people and look to pass advantages to their children, also risks perpetuating these issues and producing an elite that is sealed from the rest of society.

Educational inequality continues to play a major role in dismissive attitudes towards working people. Whilst education alone cannot solve issues that are caused by declining economic dignity, tackling this inequality and the snobbery that it helps create remain key elements to building a more cohesive society.

LEFT BEHIND FROM THE BEGINNING

I had first-hand experience of the way in which our education system leaves working-class young people behind.

I grew up in the shadow of the closure of Consett's once mighty steelworks, with the town suffering from the highest rate of unemployment in Western Europe. I attended the local comprehensive, which overlooked the site of the old steelworks, so the closure of the works was very much a literal and metaphorical backdrop. Plenty of my classmates had parents who were out of work, and the school had to deal with a variety of social and economic issues. Many good and inspiring teachers often found they were running just to keep up, and only about 12 per cent of the sixteen-year-olds I went to school with could achieve five or more good GCSEs. The national average at the time was 45 per cent and is now about 60 per cent. There was little talk of university at the school, probably just as our privately educated peers were having high expectations drummed into them.

I saw so many bright, brilliant people go on to low-paid, insecure jobs. Many were undoubtedly more gifted than some of those I met when I moved to London, but a large number of the latter unquestionably felt that they had been lifted into professional jobs by 'meritocracy' and their own talent. As Iain Macleod famously said, my schoolmates were being told to 'stand on their own two feet' when the ground on which they stood had been taken away. The education system didn't do enough for the brilliant people I went to school with, and, despite some welcome reforms, it clearly continues to hold back too many people from working-class backgrounds.

The educational abandonment of the working class starts at an early age and from there gets wider. Research conducted in Montreal found a clear correlation between parental income and childhood stress. Research from the Joseph Rowntree Trust suggested: 'There are big differences in cognitive, and social and emotional development between children growing up in poor families, and those from better-off backgrounds. This gap grows even wider by the age of five.'[4] Five-year-olds from the most advantaged groups are a year ahead in vocabulary compared to the most disadvantaged groups. Such an early lag has been shown to have lasting consequences: children who have poor language skills at the age of five are twice as likely to be unemployed in their mid-thirties.

This class divide grows as children get older. A number of studies have shown that the 'attainment gap' between rich and poor widens by the time a child turns seven, and grows wider still by the age of eleven. By the time young people take their GCSEs, candidates from the richest families score thirty-three percentile points higher than young people from the poorest families. In terms of development, those in receipt of free school meals are almost twenty months behind other pupils by the end of secondary school. Only 1 per cent of schools in the least deprived areas are described as 'inadequate' and 8 per cent as 'needing improvement' in Ofsted school inspections. By contrast, this is the case for 38 per cent of schools in the most deprived areas, with some 11 per cent being described as inadequate.

THE WHITE WORKING CLASS – FALLING FURTHER BEHIND

Praiseworthy progress has been made by some groups within society, but white working-class young people continue to be left behind. For those sixteen-year-olds on free school meals, children of black African, Bangladeshi and Chinese ancestry have made notable and welcome strides, with each group showing performance improvements of over 20 per cent in the ten years from 2006. Children from Chinese and Indian backgrounds now perform better than any other group. The notable group that has failed to make any progress and looks to have fallen further behind is the white working class.

Almost a decade ago, Ofsted talked about the 'stubbornly low outcomes [of white working-class boys] that show little signs of improvement'.[5] A Labour minister vowed to tackle the issue in 2008. In 2014, the head of school inspections identified that white working-class children were 'consistently the lowest performing group in the country',[6] and Theresa May famously raised the issue in her doorstep speech in Downing Street when she became Prime Minister.

Despite all this apparent political interest, it remains a more intractable issue than ever. Perhaps this is because, as the former head of UCAS suggests, the problem 'always got a few headlines, [but] where it never got any traction at all was in policy-making in government. I began to think that the subject of white boys is just too difficult for them'.[7] A noble few politicians, such as Robert Halfon, MP for Harlow, have consistently raised the issue and offered potential solutions, but for most politicians the issue has long been filed under the 'too difficult, too controversial' category. But only 24 per cent of white British boys and 32 per cent of white British girls on free school meals achieve five or more good GCSEs. This means that white working-class boys represent by far the worst performing major ethnic group, and white working-class girls are also the lowest performing female ethnic group. There are a number of potential reasons for this – declining social capital, lack of sufficient role models, lack of political will to push resources into the issue – but it is clear that the underperformance of white working-class boys should no longer be a peripheral issue. The problem is stark and tragic and clearly not one we can merely mouth platitudes about any longer.

HIGHER EDUCATION:
SHARPENING THE DIVIDE?

Such a long-lasting educational gap should give us pause for thought as a nation. Because of the tilted structure of education and the economy, the gap also deprives young people of opportunity and a voice. As journalist David Goodhart has argued, the only route to the 'zone of safety and success' in the modern economy is via university, because the multiple ladders to success that were once in place have been replaced with a single ladder.[8] This means that young people left behind by the education system from an early age continue to be left behind throughout their lives.

Despite best intentions, the middle class continues to dominate universities, with private-school pupils eight times more likely than white working-class boys to attend university. Although there has been an increase in working-class young people going to university, the greatest beneficiaries of the expansion of university education have been the middle classes, making stratification even more pronounced. There remains a direct correlation between economic advantage and the ability to attend university, with some academics arguing that university expansion has benefited the 'not-so-bright middle class' rather than the academically able members of the working class.[9]

The fact that many of the top universities still have very

few students from working-class backgrounds has led some observers to point out that elements of higher education remain 'a steeply hierarchical and stratified system with working-class students, for the most part, clustered in the low status, poorly resourced, institutions'.[10]

As the government's own Social Mobility Commission has acknowledged, 'The more educationally advantaged a child's background, the more likely they are to go to university'.[11] Whereas some 45 per cent of eighteen-year-olds now attend university, that figure falls to 29 per cent for those on free school meals and to only 5 per cent for the top third of universities. For white working-class boys on free school meals, though, the figures are even more shaming, with only 13 per cent going on to university. This is half of the proportion of black Caribbean boys on free school meals who go to university, and around a quarter of the proportion of Indian males on free school meals. More than half of UK universities have fewer than 5 per cent of white young people from working-class families as part of their intake. Contrast this with the 85 per cent from private schools who go on to university and the societal division becomes crystal clear: the more advantaged a child's background, the more likely they are to go to university.

There are important reasons for the low number of white working-class boys attending university, and they include, in some cases, a culture of low expectations, a lack of social capital and an early disengagement from the schooling system. But a lack of serious prioritisation of the issue by both policy-makers and universities has also been important. Whereas most institutions set diversity targets, as a report by King's College London suggests, 'Few [universities] formally document the widening participation activities they are targeting specifically at this group.' Another recent report showed that only two institutions in the country mentioned white working-class males as a group that should be explicitly measured.

For many universities and in many parts of British life, the concept of diversity tends to stop when it comes to class and particularly white working-class boys, who are regarded by some as having benefited on account of both their race and their gender. Indeed, politicians who have addressed the issue, such as Halfon, have found themselves accused of racism for even raising the topic. As we'll see, this is part of a wider systemic issue that risks further marginalising the working class. An age in which an emphasis is placed on concepts such as 'hegemonic masculinity' and 'white privilege' is unlikely to be one that prioritises the underperformance of white working-class males.

A CONTINUING DISPARITY OF ESTEEM

The issues around higher education entry might matter less if society had a larger number of well-paid, skilled

jobs in manufacturing and a viable, highly esteemed vocational route. Sadly, that is not the case. The economy is
now organised in a way that substantially favours those
going to university. Professions like accountancy, law
and journalism, which once had a non-graduate route
and indeed were predominantly non-graduate up until
the 1970s and '80s, have all but shut down that route. A
study that looked at accountancy in particular found that
'accountants tend to come from privileged backgrounds
and those who qualified with Big Four firms possess more
economic, social and cultural capital than those who qual-
ify with other firms'.[12] Although the Big Four accountancy
firms have done more than many professions to diversify
in terms of social background, even their efforts so far
seem to have had little real impact.

As we have seen, the two-tier economy that has fuelled
the new snobbery has been accompanied by a two-tier
education system that has intensified it. Difference in
esteem between working-class and professional jobs is
accompanied by a gulf in esteem between academic and
technical education. Almost 70 per cent of respondents in
one Cedefop poll said they felt that technical education
was for those with 'low grades' and only a quarter said
they would recommend vocational education to young
people. The perception of the sector as being one for
those who 'fail at school' continues to have a drag on any
attempts to achieve parity of esteem.

Vocational education remains popular 'in principle', but as the Social Mobility Commission argues, it continues to be the option for 'other people'. Few professional parents would countenance the vocational route for their own children. There has also been a long-term funding disparity between the two; technical education has been consistently underfunded and successive governments have failed to meet the promises they have made to improve it. Meanwhile, according to Onward research, the number of low-value higher education courses has shot up, with around a quarter of students now studying degrees that bring them no 'earnings premium'. An overinflated higher education sector and the continued lack of an esteemed and embedded technical route leads to an unequal distribution of prestige and reward and contributes to a divided nation.

Twice as many young people from poorer backgrounds are studying in further education (FE) colleges than in school sixth forms. These FE colleges have seen considerable funding cuts in the past few decades, with a 16 per cent cut in real terms in the past decade and far more public spending on those young people taking A-Levels than those going down the further education route.[13] FE colleges have had to cut back on their number of courses, increase class sizes and reduce links with companies.

Funding to technical education in the UK is 23 per cent less than academic education and well below the OECD average. In her review of further education, Baroness Wolf described the disparity of funding between the two routes as 'unsustainable' and 'deeply inegalitarian'.[14] The continual preference for higher education and A-Levels over further education and technical skills again stands as testament to government in the interests of the better off that was discussed in the Introduction. The boosting of apprenticeships in recent years has been a welcome development, with their numbers increasing from 167,000 in 2003, to 280,000 in 2010 and almost 500,000 in 2017. This, along with the introduction of 'T-Levels', provides a strong and important base to improve the UK's technical education, but there is still much more to be done.

Contrast Britain's approach to that in continental Europe. In Germany and Scandinavia, vocational education is embedded within companies and the school curriculum and has parity of esteem with academic education. Most middle-class parents in the UK would object to their children going down the vocational route, whereas in northern Europe, technical education is seen as a prestigious and valuable path to a well-paid and respected job. Almost half of the German population, including several members of Angela Merkel's Cabinet, have a technical qualification. Germany's highly productive, highly skilled workforce is partially a product of a system that holds Vocational Education and Training (VET) in high esteem. Scandinavian countries also have a similar 'dual learning' model, which around half of young people participate in. The same countries have some of the best rates of people from poorer backgrounds gaining professional jobs. In the UK, parental income has twice as much impact on the future earnings of children than is the case in Scandinavia. This finding led the UK's Social Mobility Commission to observe that in the UK 'it pays to be privileged'.[15]

A rush to expand higher education has been important, but it has also perpetuated the idea that those who don't attend university are less worthwhile and less worthy of economic, social or political respect. Such a shift has also hollowed out many towns as talented young people leave to attend university and never return, perpetuating the 'escape' mentality. This has also led to a more stratified society between those who have university degrees and those who do not.

THE EDUCATIONAL DIVIDE THAT LEADS TO A DIVIDED SOCIETY

In a society and economy that values degrees and a university education above all other qualifications, graduates are likely to gain social capital and status from their education in a way that non-graduates do not. The culture of leaving town to go to a residential university not only creates a brain drain; it also means that friendship groups are much less likely to be mixed. As time goes on, educated people are more likely to associate only with other educated people, to live in the same parts of town as other graduates, to marry other educated people and to pass on their advantages to their children. In this way, university education and the social capital and respect it brings with it has become almost a birthright of the professional class.

Academics call this process 'assortative mating' or 'associative mating', which, as cultural commentator David Brooks has pointed out, has meant that marriage announcements in major newspapers have started to look like law firm mergers. A number of studies have shown that recent decades have been marked by a decline in marriages across educational divides and that this might also have contributed to a rise in income inequality.

As this educational elite has become more self-insulated, the distance between social groups has become greater than at any time since the Second World War, with 'class mixing' inside or outside the workplace much less likely than in previous decades. The oligarchic elite has become as self-perpetuating as any of its aristocratic predecessors. Christopher Lasch has noted that the 'upper middle class, the heart of the new professional and managerial elites, is defined by a way of life that distinguishes it, more and more unmistakably, from the rest of the population'. On a crude level, this stratification builds society into silos, which produces a lack of understanding or sympathy. When combined with a belief that economic advancement is due to talent alone, this can result in a corrosive disdain for the less educated. The failure of generations of politicians to improve the educational performance of the white working class, combined with decisions to venerate university as the sole route to success, has helped to create a modern version of Disraeli's fear of 'two nations between whom there is no intercourse and no sympathy; who are as ignorant of each other's habits, thoughts and feelings as if they were dwellers in different zones, or inhabitants of different planets'.

Old-style snobbery continues to cast an ugly shadow over many of the universities that continue to be bastions of the middle class. The Social Mobility Commission has found that 'elitism and class-based segregation exist in many universities around the country'. Mockery of regional accents and issues with a lack of pre-existing networks has also been shown to hold working-class young people back. Some of the worst examples of this snobbery have been seen at an elite institution at the emotional core of what was industrial working-class England. The rugby team at Durham University was condemned for organising a miners' strike party with a dress code of 'flat caps, filth and a general disregard for personal safety'.[16] The university is only yards away from the heartbeat of old, industrial working-class Britain but draws almost 40 per cent of its students from private schools. Local students from working-class backgrounds have reported a 'toxic culture' towards them, with one reporting that what started with a mocking and mimicking of her accent 'persistently became the butt of jokes about coal mining and started to get called feral because I was local, [meaning the abuse] started to feel malicious'.[17] There have recently been a flood of reports about offensively titled 'rolling in the muck' competitions between privileged students (self-described 'posh lads') who share stories in WhatsApp groups of having sex with 'the poorest girls on campus'.[18]

'IT PAYS TO BE PRIVILEGED'

Even for working-class graduates, the 'professions' remain a largely closed shop, with the majority of people working in professional occupations coming from professional backgrounds. Working-class backgrounds remain seriously underrepresented in business, in the media and in quangos and government bodies. The government's Social Mobility Commission says the 'better off are nearly 80 per cent more likely to end up in professional jobs than those from a working-class background', and those from a working-class background in professional jobs earn 17 per cent less than those from privileged backgrounds.[19]

In their excellent book *The Class Ceiling: Why It Pays*

to Be Privileged, Friedman and Laurison have noted that this class pay gap, which even exists for working-class students who have graduated from Oxbridge, 'is not explained away by conventional indicators of "merit". As they argue:

> When even institutions like Oxford and Cambridge ... do not wash away the advantages of class privilege ... this surely constitutes a stark rejoinder to even the most strident believers in Britain's meritocracy. The class pay gap represents a powerful and previously unobserved axis of inequality that clearly demands urgent attention.[20]

Overall, those from working-class backgrounds earn 24 per cent less than those from professional backgrounds, and this gap has stayed stubbornly large since it was first measured almost two decades ago. The pay gap exists in professional and non-professional jobs, and it is even bigger for the non-privately educated, with privately educated men being paid 34 per cent more than those from the state system. According to research by the London School of Economics, if you are a working-class graduate with a first-class degree, you're less likely to land an elite job than a middle-class graduate with a 2:2.

Class remains a secondary diversity factor for both the university and the private sector; even though class remains the key predictor of economic success, it continues to be ignored in many discussions of diversity. The *Harvard Business Review* points out that 'most big companies today have diversity and inclusion programs focused on issues of race and gender in the workplace. But in these initiatives, very few companies include socioeconomic class as a dimension.'[21] Many academic and business articles talk at length about the importance of diversity without even mentioning class as a factor. It's possibly not accidental that a focus on socio-economic class might be more troubling for the comfort-zone graduate silos than a focus on other areas. And the marginalisation of class is even more extreme when white working-class boys, excluded from most diversity schemes, are concerned.

Educational marginalisation of the working class has substantial societal implications that can't be ignored. As we have discussed, it has led to a more stratified society than any we have seen in the modern era. As well as contributing to social division, we know that an education system that leaves too many working-class young people behind also contributes directly to the new snobbery through educationism, defined by the *Journal of Experimental Social Psychology* as the implicit bias of the educated against the less educated. Tackling the new snobbery through improved education and rethinking diversity to incorporate socio-economic class would be an important way of ensuring that it no longer pays to be privileged.

TOWARDS A PRO-WORKER EDUCATION POLICY

The educational exclusion of many working-class people, which starts with lower birth weight and ends with only 13 per cent of white working-class boys attending university, has profound societal and economic consequences. It deepens social stratification and feelings of snobbery based on levels of education. The new snobbery that we have seen played out in politics is underlined by educational differences and a growing sense amongst educated professionals that people with fewer qualifications are less worthy of esteem and respect. Such a divide is deeply damaging for society. We should consider steps both to prioritise improved results from those who are being left behind and to create an alternative technical route which has equal esteem to the academic path.

CHAPTER THREE

THE RISE OF 'WOKE' AND THE MARGINALISATION OF WORKING-CLASS CONCERNS

'By failing to problematize whiteness … literature obscures the privileges that working-class whites can access.'

JEREMY BOHONOS, WITH ONE OF SEVERAL EXAMPLES OF 'CRITICAL THEORY' BEING USED TO MINIMISE THE BARRIERS CREATED BY SOCIO-ECONOMIC ISSUES.[1]

'At no point did Labour "desert" the working class. But a section of it deserted us last night, and I am not going to flinch from stating that in the places it did so there is now a toxic narrative of nativism and xenophobia.'

PAUL MASON[2]

In recent years, a new form of trenchant radicalism has emerged. The growth of identity politics, often given the shorthand of 'wokeism', has transformed the priorities of many progressives, resulting in a marginalisation of working-class concerns. It has also transformed much of the cultural narrative, particularly at elite level, with many wealthy white radicals ready to symbolically prove their virtue and condemn great swathes of the working class as 'deplorables'.

For most supporters, the starting point for this type of politics is an entirely praiseworthy one – that all citizens should be able to live their lives without discrimination or prejudice. They are also right to focus on removing obstacles facing black people, women and LGBT citizens, which, in areas like criminal justice, continue to be considerable. Sadly, the extremes of identity politics often ignore these issues of substance in favour of symbolism, and they risk belittling decades of progress in the UK in an attempt to see prejudice always and everywhere.

We should be proud of the advances that we have made in race relations and gender equality in recent decades but also accept that there is more to do. Two out of the four Great Offices of State are held by MPs of Indian heritage; gay people can now marry; and open acts of bigotry are no longer regarded as acceptable. Some 40 per cent of NHS consultants are from ethnic minority backgrounds. Whilst celebrating this, we should also accept that much more needs to be done to tackle the significant hurdles that BAME people still face in British society. This is not what the identity-based orthodoxy does. Instead, it has created a culture where sloganeering and middle-class self-flagellation have replaced a solution-based discussion about concrete and important issues.

Where the end goal was once, correctly, the elimination of prejudice and a move to a colour-blind society, modern identity politics seems to thrive on division and difference. Often, an excessive policing of language and a desire to maximise differences risks making a virtue out of such division and ignoring the importance of common bonds and solidarity. Identity politics is too often an 'all or nothing' concept that maximises conflict and eschews moderation. As David Brooks has argued, the main issue with wokeness is that 'it doesn't inspire action; it freezes it ... To make a problem seem massively intractable is to inspire separation – building a wall between you and the problem – not a solution.'[3]

By seeing differences as defining and virtuous, and prejudice as inevitable and intractable, woke politics risks baking in division. Emphasising separation over integration and solidarity risks decades of progress (although there is always more to be done). By promoting self-flagellation and symbolism over solutions, woke politics seems almost certain to promote disappointment and make too little difference to the real problems. Indeed, by aggressively policing language and adopting a harsh censoriousness, wokeness introduces a new sense of intolerance. A sucking up of time into debates about street names, statues and wartime leaders represents a diversion of energy that could be focused on delivering concrete change that improves people's lives. At its worst, wokeism favours concerns like language over more material concerns that impact how people live on a daily basis.

Identity politics also explicitly prioritises issues, but in that list of priorities, the concerns of the working class are relegated or forgotten. The barriers facing people because of class are ignored, and this also does a disservice to working-class people from ethnic minority backgrounds. Some concepts that have emerged out of the woke canon, such as 'white privilege', risk not only relegating working-class concerns but also *blaming* some working-class people for not making the most of their apparent privilege and suggesting that they only have themselves to blame for their economic situation. It regards issues like the poor educational performance of white working-class boys as unimportant, whilst giving the wealthy the ability to illustrate their virtue without taking into account their economic privilege.

This brand of politics sees large swathes of the working class not as the backbone of society but as *the problem and the obstacle to progress* in a debate which advocates have deliberately hyper-charged. For middle-class activists, the cultural conservatism of many in working-class towns puts workers beyond the pale, in a Maoist approach that sees identity as our only defining characteristic.

At its most extreme, identity politics has allowed

barriers faced by working-class people to be sidelined by new 'identity'-based ideas that have emerged from largely middle-class scholars in largely middle-class universities, with dizzying rules of acceptable language that are policed and frequently altered by the highly educated. Rather than promoting lasting solutions to prejudice and discrimination, 'wokeness' actually gives greater power to a highly educated elite over defining societal priorities and acceptable language, whilst relegating class concerns and attaching blame (and even shame) to parts of the working class for their own situations.

THE MARCH OF THE MIDDLE-CLASS SCHOLARS

As we've noted, despite attempts to 'widen participation', universities continue to be largely the preserve of the middle class. These same universities have been at the heart of developing the woke orthodoxy. This has seen so-called 'scholar activists' push working-class concerns to the periphery and embrace a movement by which 'social crusaders portray themselves as the sole and righteous champions of social and moral progress'.[4] Some entire departments in UK universities are now given over to scholar activism. A form of snobbery is inevitable in this brand of academia and politics that sees the world according to an unarguable state of enlightened and revealed insight that can only be understood using the explanations of the activist scholars.

An intolerance of alternative viewpoints has been at the heart of this movement, effectively representing an attempt by middle-class academics to set the terms of acceptable debate. This matters because the rise of this form of identity-obsessed radicalism has become instrumental in marginalising working-class concerns and creating a culture that legitimises snobbery and elite disdain. Such a culture will then inform working environments for years to come as students become professionals who recruit in their own attitudinal image.

Wokeism is a development of postmodernism, with its emphasis on identifying and dismantling power structures and rejecting traditional metanarratives. It has moved to become 'applied critical theory', with a focus on privilege and biases. Above all, these ideas represent a rejection of Enlightenment values; an emphasis on power structure; a focus on the power of language; and a rejection of borders, nations and the West. Identity politics sees white, heteronormative and patriarchal power dynamics as being always and everywhere, always providing advantages for white, Western men and representing immovable disadvantages to others. It's a nihilistic concept, built entirely on seeing an ever-present bias, ignoring progress that has been made and providing no positive vision.

The concept of identity politics has long since

entrenched itself in many sociology, psychology and anthropology departments across the country. A whole new range of subjects has also grown with an explicit focus on pushing these concepts. In 2020, an angry letter condemning a black government minister for expressing doubts about critical race theory was signed by academics representing a wide range of recently established disciplines, including the near ubiquitous subjects of gender studies and black studies, plus other more niche disciplines such as cultural equity, ableism, inclusive education, race- and practice-based social justice and postcolonial studies.

These new disciplines have proved helpful for TV producers looking for academics willing to denigrate British history. One lecturer was wheeled out to promote the theory that Churchill was 'a racist' and 'worse than Hitler'. He also described 'whiteness' as a 'psychosis'.[5] Elsewhere, a lecturer in women's studies, with a speciality in vulnerability and gender, said that she hoped Oxford didn't develop a Covid vaccine as it would give the UK a 'world's saviour' complex.[6]

Wokesim hasn't just impacted new academic disciplines; many traditional subjects have been revolutionised too. History, for example, has been particularly badly hit, with many taking on the mantle of Edward Said, the high priest of postcolonialism, who argued that 'history can be unmade and rewritten'.[7] In Britain, this means taking a relentlessly negative approach to British history, which is to be seen as one of almost total shame and which we should apologise for or be embarrassed about. Any pride in this history is regarded as evidence of an innate bigotry combined with a lack of enlightened education. Trevor Phillips has argued that the new approach represents 'a gross caricature that distorts our rich and complex history'.[8] It ignores the complexity that should be at the heart of history, substitutes propaganda and ideology for proper academic analysis (see the nonsense view that the British Empire was 'worse than Nazis', propagated by attention-seeking professors at Churchill College, Cambridge), seeks to diminish achievements like the abolition of the slave trade and flies in the face of the majority of public opinion, which sees British history as something to be proud of.[9] Many of the proponents of the new, decolonised history are ideologues and propagandists and should be treated as such.

Any relativism about historical circumstances is being replaced by a monist worldview that sees through a binary prism of pure right and pure wrong. As history is redefined, it leads to the nonsense of universities having to rename buildings named after former Prime Minister William Gladstone, ostensibly for fear of causing offence. University authorities, along with other bodies, have become so eager to please a vocal but small minority of radicals that they have lost sight of what is reasonable or proportionate.

An increasing number of universities have also become committed to 'decolonising the curriculum', defined by Keele University's 'Manifesto for Decolonizing' as 'a paradigm shift from a culture of exclusion and denial to the making of space for other political philosophies and knowledge systems' and representing a shift away from 'Western-centric worldviews'.[10] The National Union of Students continues to push for an entire 'decolonising of the university', which represents 'a change in what is studied and how it is studied'.[11] Universities have begun to act on such demands, with reading lists and other materials being based more on 'representation' and 'removing whiteness' than academic rigour. Some universities have even considered removing English classics such as Chaucer from the English literature curriculum on account of their 'whiteness' and 'Eurocentricity'. A 2018 book called *Decolonising the University* suggested this should extend to philosophy, arguing that philosophy 'remains a bastion of Eurocentrism, whiteness in general and white heteronormative male structural privilege in particular'.[12] Even maths and science can't escape the avalanche: one author has promised to draw 'on the insights of higher-dimensional mathematics to reveal a transformative new way of talking about the patriarchy'.[13]

Academics promoting these theories are self-described 'scholar activists' who see the divide between scholarship, learning and activism as no longer relevant and regard 'changing society' to be as important as imparting knowledge.

Scholars, first in the United States and shortly after in the UK, have increasingly seen their work as being part of a 'powerful force for change'. One academic argued that

> part of being active citizens involves challenging our students to do and be more ... there is a need for academics as part of their normal working lives to ... even at times become members of political and advocacy organisations. Rigorous research carried out 'for a cause' must again be accepted as legitimate knowledge generation.[14]

A professor of social justice at the University of Birmingham likewise proudly tweeted that her 'job as an academic is to question, challenge, dismantle and disrupt. And to teach my students to do the same.'[15] *Take It to the Streets* was the fitting name for a collection of essays that brought together academics wrestling with how academia could help contribute to protest movements.

Why does this matter for the purposes of this book? Surely trends in academia are, literally, just academic? The truth is these avant-garde theories aren't limited to universities, and they are playing a direct role in the marginalisation of working-class concerns. The activist who coined the term 'intersectionality' (the division of people into more and more detailed and interlinked identities, unlikely to include class) made clear that her goal was to develop a 'concept linking contemporary politics with postmodern theory'.[16] And she has been successful beyond her wildest dreams, with the politics of identity long surpassing the politics of class on the centre-left and legitimising snobbery as it advances.

Another modern academic has described intersectionality and associated genres as 'an analytical framework in the process of reaching maximum salience across academe, the nonprofit sector and politics'.[17] In reaching 'maximum salience', it has further entrenched negative perceptions of the undereducated and provided a theoretical underpinning for such views. The irony of highly educated, upper-middle-class scholars pushing the concept of privilege seems to be lost on the academics doing the pushing.

Even many of the protest movements associated with the new radicalism are overwhelmingly middle class. Eighty-five per cent of Extinction Rebellion protesters were graduates, and two thirds described themselves as middle class. Harry Mount has described this group as 'Econians – the public-school boys and girls who rule the wokerati world'.[18]

The growth of 'woke' has led to a new form of

pop-culture politics, in which the ideas that advance from academia, generally in the USA, become easily Insta-grammable memes about identity, which make discussing complex issues related to class much more difficult. Socio-economic barriers are less likely to be acknowledged in such an environment, especially when ideas like white privilege make such discussion more complex. It also rep-resents middle-class academics developing new bound-aries of acceptable discussion that non-graduates will simply have to accept.

MADE IN THE USA?

Orwell famously said that the left-wing elite of his time got their 'cookery from Paris and their opinions from Moscow', whereas it's clear that today's elites get their cookery from Whole Foods and their academic theories from the USA. The extremes of wokeism represent the worst element of a desire to copy America and, ironically, are a form of American cultural imperialism. If a crazy idea is articulated on a university campus in America, there's little doubt that it will be regurgitated by British radicals a few months later.

As *The Atlantic*'s Helen Lewis memorably put it, 'the world is trapped in America's culture war' after America 'won the internet … and now makes us all speak its lan-guage', with memes and mottos becoming global social media trends, with little concern for local differences.[19] Importing slogans wholesale from America is counter-productive. The United States and the UK have very different issues (we have no armed police, for example) and different experiences (there is no British equivalent of Jim Crow, and the UK was the first major power fighting to abolish the slave trade, using its navy to do so at the same time as slavery continued in the US). To suggest the two are comparable is to do the UK a disservice. Rather than considering the specific issues facing BAME people in the UK, the mass importation of ideas from the US, via social media or a global media culture, risks reducing discussion of important issues to superficiality. 'Made in the USA' slogans are no substitute for actual policy proposals that address the uniquely British experience. Ethnic minority people in the UK, for example, are more likely to be in low-paid work than the population as a whole. The rate of unemployment amongst black people is higher than that of any other group, and black men are nine times more likely than other groups to be subjected to police stop and search. Addressing these kinds of issues will make a more profound difference to people's lives than endless discussions about Empire or street names – arguments that often seem to exist solely in order to boost the profile of activist academics.

This copyism of the US was taken to an extreme when parts of the British left started campaigning to 'defund the police' only a few months after standing on a manifesto that promised to massively increase the policing budget. The modern left often lacks subtlety or originality as much as it lacks an authentic sympathy with the working class. It reached absurd levels when a desire to copy the reasonable campaign to topple statues in the American South led to bizarre claims that Grey's monument and statues of Gladstone should be torn down. Whilst basing these claims for statue removal on links to slavery, the real driving force behind the British woke left was to copy the very different movement in the USA. Earl Grey was a steadfast reformer and opponent of the slave trade; Gladstone also opposed the slave trade and described Britain's engagement in it as our 'foulest crime'. That is before we consider the folly of judging politicians from centuries ago using the standards of today. Kneejerk, copyist instincts to do 'something' should not be a substitute for a proper understanding of history.

Possibly most importantly, this approach, which sees history as a contemporary battleground and citizens as nothing more than expressions of group identity, is also self-defeating and will make the country more polarised, whilst doing very little to tackle economic and social problems facing black people or to genuinely further the cause of racial and gender equality. Journalist George Packer has noted a habit on the left of seeing people 'as molecules dissolved in vast and undifferentiated ethnic and racial solutions without individual agency [that] is both analytically misleading and politically self-defeating, doing actual harm to the cause of equality'.[20] Such a myopic approach to identity risks avoiding the progress that the UK has made – for example, the UK has more ethnic minority Cabinet ministers than the rest of Europe combined, and 6 per cent of junior doctors are black, compared to 3 per cent of the population – instead seeing politics solely through a lens of identity and minimising the solidarity needed for progress.

The logic of some of the most extreme of the woke warriors is ultra-divisive and risks seeing society merely through the prism of racial division. One of the most vocal academic proponents of identity politics in the UK even argued that 'the biggest mistake we [black people] make in Britain is that we really do try to integrate into society' going on to argue that this undermined his desire for a distinctly racial identity.[21] Such an approach clearly risks creating division by seeing society only through a single prism, undermining all the gains that society has made and even creating what some have described as a 'woke Powellism'.

The former head of the Commission for Racial Equality in the UK is excoriating about what he describes as intolerant wokeism and those who 'claim to be the allies of the oppressed yet have no time to listen to their real priorities. They purport to seek greater diversity, yet require all women or all ethnic minorities to share their view or be branded quislings.' He laments the fact that the 'woke' movement is consistently led by middle-class white people who are more drawn to symbolism and self-flagellation than achieving practical remedies tackling structural issues like housing, policing, education and jobs. When 'social media warriors move on to the next fashionable cause, minorities will still be less likely to win the top jobs, and women will still be the victims of violence. The only thing that will have changed is the bitterness of a generation whose idealism was betrayed.'[22] It is incumbent on all of those who care about societal solidarity to tackle these structural issues and do more to build a multi-racial solidarity.

RADICALISM OF THE RICH?

The left has gone from being full-throated supporters of the working class to seeing them as either low down the list of priorities or as an embodiment of the 'wrong kind of politics'. One of the early counterculture 'bibles' which had an important influence on the new left even described blue-collar workers as the 'arch opponents of the new consciousness'.[23] As former Democrat presidential candidate Andrew Yang observed, this has created a situation where many are 'more concerned about policing various cultural issues than improving the [working-class] way of life'.[24] The rise of 'woke' has coincided with a new kind of radicalism, largely driven by the middle class and sometimes the very wealthy, which neglects socio-economic barriers and all too often relegates the white working class to the bottom of the pile.

As we have seen, the views of the 'uneducated' are all too often sneered at by contemporary elitists. Their reverence for tradition, country and self-governance is seen as parochial and old fashioned and any support for controlled immigration is immediately labelled as racist. Aris Roussinos has observed how a new radicalism led by 'high-status' individuals 'prioritises the global over the local, and denigrates the nation-state as a backward relic of an oppressive past [and has] become the dominant value system of the Western professional classes'. As the 'political ideology associated with the values of celebrities, international business travellers, NGO professionals and journalists', the worldview has 'acquired the glossy sheen of high social status'.[25]

For proponents of this way of thinking, it is not an ideology they are holding but the only moral and legitimate worldview, opposition to which must be driven by chauvinism and small-mindedness at best, and by reactionary fanaticism and racism at worst. In driving this perception, high-status professionals have attempted to set the terms of debate and acceptable discourse and in doing so diminish working-class concerns to those of parochial

King Canutes, trying to hold back the waves of inevitable progress.

The rise of wokeism has taken the dismissal of working-class voices by privileged elites even further, with the development of theories that reject the white working class and diminish their claim to prioritisation. This represents a political disempowerment of the working class that risks becoming baked into elite thinking, leaving the working class even further behind. The growth of identity politics has moved far beyond the important concept that there is no place in British society for prejudice. As a society we still have to go further to tackle racism and discrimination in criminal justice, in the jobs market and in housing, health and education. Sadly, too much of contemporary identity politics focuses on broad gestures, sweeping slogans and snapshot judgements, rather than really addressing the complex issues facing modern Britain.

Wokeism is a belief, which has become an article of faith amongst much of the managerial elite, that group identity, notably race, sexuality and gender (but not nationality if the nation is Western) is the most important and defining form of identity. This is then used to consider various types of historical or contemporary disadvantage or prejudice as defining the experience of that group. Under this scenario, certain groups are oppressed and other groups are oppressors. In all cases, white males are seen as the oppressor group. Group identity is certainly viewed as more important than British national identity, which is regarded as anachronistic and reactionary. The dominant ideology is identity-based and designed to emphasise differences and divide rather than unite us.

This theory reaches its apotheosis with the concept of white privilege, defined as the inherent privileges possessed by white people in a society marked by prejudice. This is supported by an idea described as critical race theory, which examines society and culture using the lens of race. This argues that special privileges in society are enjoyed by white people, or the 'white, heteronormative patriarchy' to use the jargon.

The concept of white fragility, developed by a wealthy diversity consultant, self-described in her own book as the 'new racial-sheriff in town', argues that white people in Western societies all are inherently privileged and inherently, psychologically racist. Apparently 'all members of society are socialised to participate in the system of racism ... all white people benefit from racism regardless of intentions'.[26] For her, this also includes Jewish people, which is a staggering statement after centuries of oppression. John McWhorter, a professor at Columbia University, memorably described the concept of white fragility as one designed 'to make certain educated white readers feel better about themselves ... [driven by] an elaborate and pitilessly dehumanizing condescension toward black people'.[27] And as journalist Matt Taibbi argues, the absurdly simplistic concept succeeds only in putting race at the centre of our identities and making it more difficult for society to come together.

These theories are at best ludicrously simplistic, and at worst divisive and destructive. The unsophisticated nature of the concept can be boiled down to the fact that it views identity as the only important factor in society; white privilege holds the blatantly false idea that this privilege is somehow spread evenly through society. A white banker does not have the same level of privilege as a white factory worker, but the notion of white privilege suggests that both benefit equally from their oppressor status. It holds that a wealthy black Old Etonian is less privileged than a white man in Barnsley working several jobs in order to stay above the poverty line. The experience of the white working class, from the coal mines to the Somme, hardly equates to privilege, but fashionable theories provide a theoretical underpinning for elite sneering towards some of the economically less fortunate.

Voguish concepts such as white fragility ignore and diminish the importance of class. This is not accidental; it is in the interests of the mainly middle-class, mainly metropolitan new radicals to understate and eschew class and overstate other group differences. It suits privileged members of the professional elite to embrace a concept that minimises the importance of their social advantages in their advancement and diminishes the need for genuine sacrifice or diminution of their social standing. A politics based purely around identity reduces the white working class by exaggerating advantages gained through their whiteness and ignoring disadvantages that come from social background. And ignoring class as a structural barrier also ignores economic factors holding back poorer people from ethnic minority backgrounds. It provides intellectual cover for the professional elite to display social and political virtue, whilst also being disdainful of the white working class and largely ignoring their concerns.

For much of the upper middle class, identity politics provides the opportunity to display almost unlimited virtue, accompanied by very limited sacrifice. Prince Harry, from his $15 million compound in Los Angeles, can be much more comfortable mouthing platitudes about tackling white privilege than he would be with a politics that considered entrenched class advantages. Theirs is what Bertrand Russell memorably described as endorsing the 'superior virtues of the oppressed', without accepting the need for any self-sacrifice or internal reflection.

The people of Barnsley or Consett could probably do without being lectured about 'privilege' and inbuilt advantages by self-exiled aristocrats in a house that has sixteen bathrooms. Interventions by the ultra-rich, particularly when delivered at a distance of thousands of miles and from the comfort of Billionaires' Row, aren't hugely helpful when tackling complex problems.

In the US, Matthew Yglesias has described this as 'The Great Awokening', where shifts towards an identity politics have been driven by white, middle-class liberals, who now hold more liberal views on diversity than black or Hispanic voters. In the UK, there is evidence of a similar trend, with younger, middle-class voters much more likely to support even violent action and the removal of certain statues by force.

The concept of white privilege also ignores the issues discussed in this book – where the traditional working-class lag almost every other group educationally and suffer severe health and economic disadvantages. 'Woke' creates an implicit prioritisation, in which tackling the needs of the white working class is deprioritised, with important issues remaining unaddressed as all white people are seen as the beneficiaries of an intangible but despised 'privilege'.

A study by the American Psychological Association has shown that the concept of white privilege has had the impact of decreasing sympathy about the challenges, such as poverty, that poorer white people endure. The theory has enhanced the 'belief that poor white people have failed to take advantage of their racial privilege – leading to negative social evaluations'.[28]

The theory could also have a psychological impact on communities that already feel left behind. As Matthew Goodwin argues: 'The onset of new terms – toxic masculinity, white privilege – is actually going to become more of a problem as we send yet another signal to these communities that they are the problem.'[29] The broad expression of terms like white privilege 'strips away individual agency' and adds further hurdles to a group who already face substantial economic and social barriers.

It also provides cover for a politics that legitimises snobbish attacks on the white working class because of their so-called privilege. It has enabled scorn to be heaped on these communities from across the political spectrum, emphasised in the US by Clinton's 'basket of deplorables' and a particularly nasty attack by Kevin D, Williamson. Writing in the *National Review*, he argued that people should 'forget all your cheap theatrical Bruce Springsteen crap. Forget your sanctimony about struggling Rust Belt factory towns ... The white American underclass is in thrall to a vicious, selfish culture whose main products are misery and used heroin needles.'[30] Perhaps 'in thrall' is the most powerful term here as it makes clear the sense that the social and economic plight of these former industrial heartlands is a crisis entirely of the working class's own making. It is impossible to imagine such language being published about any social group other than the white working class.

On the left, Josh Marshall has argued that, for white

working-class communities, the 'stressor at work here is the perceived and real loss of the social and economic advantages of being white'.[31] The almost explicit argument is that white working-class areas had it coming after years of so-called privilege and that priority for public policy should be elsewhere. The snobbery towards 'chavs', described so well by left-wing commentator Owen Jones, makes clear that this shaming culture hasn't stopped at *The Atlantic*. The contempt expressed for many post-industrial communities in the aftermath of the Brexit vote was all too often wrapped in the concept that post-industrial areas had themselves to blame for economic and social decline.

THE POLICING OF LANGUAGE

The growth of identity politics has also led to a policing of language that plays a role in excluding working-class voters. It gives an extraordinarily small number of middle-class graduates the power to police what is deemed to be acceptable. A More in Common report put the number of 'Progressive Activists' in the UK at no more than 13 per cent of the population, but they have power and voice that far outweighs their numbers.

As Trevor Phillips argues: 'The rules are a moving target, driven by a bewildering array of changing sensitivities and shifting language ... Confusion abounds.'[32] Bewildering jargon is combined with increasingly explicit rules about what kind of language is and isn't acceptable, with middle-class activist academics generally setting and shifting the terms of acceptable debate. Confusing innovations, such as the word 'womxn', coined by 'intersectional activists' as 'an alternative spelling to avoid the suggestion of sexism perceived in the sequences m-a-n and m-e-n' could almost have been designed to confuse and alienate. For many radicals, correct pronouns have become more important than tackling economic disadvantage.

This is another import from the USA, where the policing of language led Bari Weiss to resign from the *New York Times*, complaining that 'truth isn't a process of collective discovery, but an orthodoxy already known to an enlightened few whose job is to inform everyone else ... the coin of our realm – language – is degraded in service to an ever-shifting laundry list of right causes'.[33] The developments also led a group of prominent writers to complain that 'a new set of moral attitudes and political commitments [have taken hold] that tend to weaken our norms of open debate and toleration of differences in favor of ideological conformity' and that the 'free exchange of information and ideas ... is daily becoming more constricted'.[34]

A constant, almost minute-to-minute shifting of labels and terminology provides the ability to police language in a way that delegitimises the views of those people who remain unaware of the moving goalposts. This makes it easier for the 'enlightened', almost exclusively from professional backgrounds, to shut off debate using words such as 'bigot' and to make sure the conversation is moved away from the priorities of the working-class. It gives greater power to today's elitists to set the terms of the debate and define what is and isn't acceptable. In doing so, they can shore up their position in the political power structure (to borrow their term), preserve their own high status and minimise the political influence of many working-class voters.

Michael Lind has described how this has become a major factor in the United States:

> The Long Island lockjaw accent has been replaced by the constantly updated 'woke' dialect of the emerging elite as a status marker … if you know what 'nonbinary' means and say 'Latinx' (a term rejected by the overwhelming majority of Americans of Latin American origin) then you are potentially eligible for membership in the new ruling class … The increasingly powerful and intolerant woke national overclass justifies its cultural iconoclasm in the name of oppressed minorities. But this is just an excuse for a top-down program of cultural imperialism by mostly white, affluent, college-educated managers and professionals and rentiers.[35]

Language as a status marker is a clear way of emphasising class differences and excluding many working-class people from the political conversation. An emphasis on language also shifts the conversation away from socio-economic factors and removes the emphasis on making material changes to improve quality of life.

TOWARDS A MULTI-RACIAL, PRO-WORKER COALITION

As we have seen, identity politics plays a triple role in minimising the political voice of working-class voters. It does this by emphasising group differences rather than economic circumstance; by stressing concepts like 'white privilege' and therefore deprioritising measures to tackle deep-seated educational and economic disadvantage; and by attempting to police language and the terms of the debate, thus legitimises snobbery and giving greater power to highly educated professionals.

It is important, though, to tackle the remnants of bigotry, racism, sexism and homophobia. Contrary to the defeatist nihilism of woke activists, we should be clear that prejudice can be defeated and the obstacles standing in the way of BAME people, women and gay people should be removed. This cannot be done via elite-led symbolism. Instead, it must be done by building a coalition that crosses sexuality, race and gender lines and accepts that the vast majority of people, regardless of identity don't want to denigrate British history nor divide the country.

CHAPTER FOUR

A CULTURE OF SNOBBERY?

'The creative class anticipates the future, while the working class tends to seek protection from it.'

RICHARD FLORIDA

'Working-class kids aren't represented. Working-class life is not referred to. It's really sad. I think it means we're going to get loads more middle-class drama. It will be middle-class people playing working-class people, like it used to be.'

JULIE WALTERS[1]

In the multiple lockdowns that impacted the UK during the Covid pandemic, there was one internet meme that went from strength to strength, becoming more 'viral' with each iteration. The photograph, called 'four lads', was a picture of four well-groomed men in their twenties, with tattoos and relatively tight clothing, enjoying a night out on a clear summer evening. They were in Birmingham, but they could just as easily have been in any town in the country. As the photo gained new life via social media, it began to tell the story of cultural attitudes towards much of working-class Britain. The vitriol was instant. Every stereotype was thrown in their direction. They were 'gammons', apparently, a little bit racist, closed-minded and almost certainly voted Leave in 2016. Others made them out to be indescribably shallow – apparently lacking the depth of their online critics. All these assumptions were made based on one photograph. Nobody had heard the 'lads'' views on anything, but the online snobs made multiple hypotheses. As one of the men said a year after the meme went viral: 'It all got a bit carried away ... Everyone was judging us.'[2] Another said that the suggestion they were 'racist and simple' was, understandably, one that stung but couldn't be 'further from the truth'. These four men, one tattoo artist and three construction workers, were portrayed, totally unfairly, as vulgar, ignorant meatheads. This isn't just an isolated example of a bored internet during lockdown. Instead, it was all too representative of an elite culture that is dismissive of working-class Britain. Culture had moved from laughing *with* the likes of the four lads to laughing *at* them.

Culture, at its best, is an important national unifier. At its peak, British culture represents what is best of the country and a real embodiment of the 'common good' value that pulls people together. Great TV, cinema, comedy, music and theatre often transcends class or other barriers, and that continues to be the case with the output of many of Britain's remarkable cultural institutions. This has never been a 'snooty' thing – from Morecambe and Wise to Lowry, to *The Pitmen Painters*, to the tradition gloriously described by Jonathan Rose's *The Intellectual Life of the British Working Classes*, working-class Britain has always contributed to this fine cultural tradition. Sadly, over recent years, the unifying element of culture risks being subsumed by the conditions that led to the resurgence of the new snobbery, reducing working-class representation in cultural industries.

Whilst great culture unites, too much contemporary comedy, in particular, regards working-class Leave voters as comedic punchbags – to be laughed at rather than with. Too much of the cultural sector is made by the metropolitan middle class for the tastes of the metropolitan middle class. Many of those from outside the major cities are either excluded or actively ridiculed. Novelist Ian McEwan's description of Brexiteers as 'a gang of angry old men, irritable even in victory' is probably an accurate picture of how many of the so-called 'creative class' regard those who voted to leave.[3]

Across the cultural landscape, there is little amplification of the working-class voice. Working-class people are likely to be misrepresented as shallow caricatures or extremities on TV or in film if they are represented at all, with far fewer representations of everyday life. This is likely to emerge because of a genuine lack of understanding or familiarity. Similarly, important cultural bodies, whether it be the BBC, the British Museum or the BFI, are lacking working-class representation at every level, meaning an attitudinal mindset that is often completely metropolitan and middle class.

This cultural misrepresentation is directly related to the political and educational factors that we discussed in previous chapters. Research shows that the creative class is more left-wing than any other part of the population, and this now equates to seeing great swathes of the working class as xenophobic or small-minded. Similarly, thanks to the walls built by educational exclusion, the creative class has little understanding of or sympathy with large segments of the white working class in particular.

Culture matters because it helps to define us as a nation and to shape perceptions. Culture didn't create the new snobbery, but in driving such attitudes about the traditional working class it risks becoming a platform for it. The concept of 'cultural capital' (the use of culture to confer social status), developed by Pierre Bourdieu, risks becoming increasingly important, as an elite looks to use culture to confer status and power and to differentiate themselves from the rest of the country.

CULTURAL MISREPRESENTATION

In much of the twentieth century, it was the snob and snobbish behaviour that was the butt of the joke. Snobs, with their overt fussiness about names for toilets and settees, were the perfect foil for humour. Evelyn Waugh's peculiar habit of walking several hundred yards from his family's Golders Green home to gain a much more glamorous NW3 postmark on letters he posted was just the kind of behaviour that was ripe for satirising. The best-known snobs in British popular culture were often lovable for it, with the audience knowing that their behaviour was so ridiculous it was laughable.

Margot's complaint in *The Good Life* about wearing a paper hat, saying, 'But… this is the *Daily Mirror*,' summed up her daft but endearing snobbery. We laughed along at Mainwaring's snobbish pretensions, knowing full well that he would always lose that game against Wilson, and we saw the snobbery of Boycie towards Del Boy as humorous because it was preposterous. Basil Fawlty's pomposity made him come a cropper when his fawning attitude to 'Lord Melbury' lured him into a con job.

In today's mainstream culture, it is all too often the snobs who are doing the laughing at working people, and it's the snobs who are writing the jokes. Comedy shows ever since the Brexit referendum have been full of dripping disdain for the stupidity and ignorance of working people. This attitude comes down to the often uniform values and backgrounds of people who work in culture – who have gone from mocking snobs to becoming them. Contempt towards great swathes of the working class became normalised (or even expected) in many circles after the Brexit vote, and this was even more exaggerated following the 2019 election. The commonly held view of 'ignorant' northerners stupidly voting against their own interests was repeated endlessly on quiz and satire shows. Programmes such as *The Mash Report* have been full of sketches and skits mocking the intelligence of northern Leave voters – another example of metropolitan authors writing for a metropolitan audience, with many of their fellow countrymen seen as the butt of the joke. Radio 4's *News Quiz* was even censured by the BBC's executive complaints unit for its attitude towards Leave voters.

In the past, at the same time as snobs were figures of fun, working-class life was portrayed realistically and constantly on TV and in light entertainment. The household names of the 1960s, '70s and '80s were all of pretty humble stock, from Michael Parkinson to Eric Morecambe. Parkinson recalled in a recent interview how amazing it was that a miner's son from Barnsley could go on to become one of the most respected interviewers in the country. It's hard to imagine such a rise today. Even much of the *Carry On* cast, that most British of creations, came from very modest backgrounds and often represented these backgrounds on the big screen.

The often plain, undramatic everyday life of many people was part of mainstream culture. John Lennon's paean to the 'working-class hero' might have sounded ludicrous coming from a tax exile, but it was a reminder that most of the British artists who changed the world in the 1960s came from modest backgrounds. From *The Likely Lads* to *Only Fools and Horses*, from *Bread* to *Auf Wiedersehen, Pet*, working-class life was sympathetically and accurately portrayed on screen. Peter Kay's creations, particularly *Phoenix Nights*, probably stand as the last in line for this kind of comedy.

This isn't to pretend there was some kind of golden age. Our popular culture is better without foul-mouthed, bigoted comedians being aired on prime time, and there's good reason why downright offensive shows like *Love Thy Neighbour* have been consigned to the dustbin of history. The clear truth, however, is that the content of culture is overwhelmingly representative of the creators of that culture. And the creators of most mainstream culture in the UK today are overwhelmingly metropolitan, middle-class graduates.

This means that, well-liked soap operas aside (and *Coronation Street* has always been a remarkably good microcosm), where popular culture represents the working class, it is often the caricature that middle classes believe of the working class. Such caricatures might be as seemingly benign as noting that rugby players are much more polite to the referee than footballers (ignoring the fact that the oval-ball game has also involved eye-gouging, testicle-grabbing and fake-blood scandals), or it could be something more insidious. TikToks mocking working-class people in the UK have become an increasingly popular part of the Chinese app, with the 'TikTok Chavs' group having millions of views and over 300,000 followers.

As Owen Jones has pointed out, cultural demonisation of the working class could be the kind of crude caricature of Vicky Pollard in *Little Britain*. That programme prompted the *Sunday Telegraph* to publish a remarkable opinion piece called 'In Defence of Snobbery', which lambasted the 'non-respectable working classes: the dole scroungers, petty criminals, football hooligans and teenage pram pushers ... there is a delicious relief to be had from laughing at them'.[4] A right-wing columnist even wrote for *The Times* that Pollard represented 'several of the great scourges of contemporary Britain ... pasty-faced lard-gutted slappers who'll drop their knickers in the blink of an eye'.[5] The facts that teenage pregnancy has been in sharp decline since the mid-1990s and that teenage drinking has also dramatically fallen haven't got in the way of this caricature taking hold.

Programmes focused on 'benefit scroungers' have also abounded, reinforcing false perceptions of working-class behaviour. This is combined with reality TV shows, which, as Beverley Skeggs has discussed, have often focused on negative stereotypes of working-class culture, such as obesity, heavy drinking, promiscuity and a perceived preference for 'bling' – a profoundly negative reduction of sophisticated working-class culture to the absurdities of *Geordie Shore*.

Some fashion brands have even used the stereotypes in crude attempts to build sales. One of the worst examples was when Puma invented a 'House of Hustle', complete with burner phones and a mocked-up crack den, to promote its trainers. H&M were also rightly criticised for selling a hoodie with the word 'Unemployed', whilst other brands drew criticism for using the phrase 'Council Estate Princess'. In all of these cases, negative and unusual behaviours have been promoted as the norm, with an overwhelmingly metropolitan cultural establishment taking crude guesses at what working-class life might be like. This represents snobbery slightly hidden under a shallow sheen of cool.

THE POLITICS OF CLASS AND CULTURE

Cultural caricatures and a lack of understanding of the lived experience of working-class groups comes from both left and right. Some on the right also seem to think that working-class voters will be first to man the barricades in the 'culture wars', often casting them as unbending in their social conservatism. Whilst true that these voters are hostile to dramatic social change, dislike lack of patriotism and attempts to denigrate British history and are opposed to the lunatic extremes of wokedom discussed in Chapter Three, it's unfair to caricature them as stern, unbending social conservatives. On gay marriage, for example, working-class voters were more supportive than other social groups. In Ireland, the only place where equal marriage was put to a public vote, the highest votes in favour were in the most working-class parts of Dublin.

Criticism of this kind of caricaturing has come from many on the left. However, the left also indulge in cultural caricaturing of their own. Across the cultural world, there is too little depiction of factory and supermarket workers, bus drivers and the like who might be struggling to make ends meet but aren't suffering a life of grinding poverty. In an attempt to make the case for these groups, cultural directors on the left often look to fetishise poverty in working-class areas and create an unrealistic Dickensisation of many working-class areas. The likes of Ken Loach, in an attempt to highlight the indignities of some welfare reforms, often reduce working-class life to one of constant degradation – as unrealistic and caricatured as the Vicky Pollard examples.

Similarly, some on the Cameronian right only seem to acknowledge working-class people in poverty. But, as James Frayne notes, most working-class people 'aren't in poverty, don't live in terrible estates and don't have "troubled families"'.[6] It's hard to forget the sight of well-heeled Tories at some of Cameron's early conferences as leader as they reported back from visits to council estates as though they had been visiting another country.

What Loach, David Walliams and Matt Lucas, some Tory 'modernisers', right-wing culture warriors and others all have in common is that they are middle-class people creating cartoons of working-class life for their own purposes. It's a top-down approach to writing and thinking, which fails to reflect reality for the simple reason that the writers just haven't lived it.

THE CHANGING COMPOSITION
OF BRITISH CULTURE

From top to bottom, cultural bodies are amongst the professions most dominated by middle-class graduates; the dominance of wealthier, metropolitan attitudes can be shown across the cultural field. *Fleabag*, for example, one of the best British comedies of recent years, tells the tale of a wealthy, middle-class Londoner, as well as being written by and starring a wealthy, middle-class Londoner. *The Night Manager*, a superb spy drama, starred three actors who had gone to the same exclusive prep school. The brilliant Julie Walters has lamented the fact that 'working-class kids aren't represented. Working-class life is not referred to. It's really sad. I think it means we're going to get loads more middle-class drama. It will be middle-class people playing working-class people, like it used to be.'[7] Ant and Dec make the point that media has become very 'London-centric' and is no longer accessible to working-class young people.[8]

Likewise, fashion has, according to Andrew Davis, 'become a rich person's job', with what Farrah Storr has described as 'a web-like matrix of barriers' to working-class people. This is a sad change from an environment where, as Adonis Kentros remembers, 'so many of the streetwear references we take for granted on the catwalks stem from the early work of brave, open-minded British designers, stylists and photographers … who came from really, really humble working-class roots … and wanted to reinterpret what was happening in their hometowns'.[9]

Artist Gary Hume has lamented that the art world has become 'just another professional option for the young and affluent'.[10] Stuart Maconie chronicles the shift from a time when in music and in the arts 'working-class kids [would] shake the world with every shake of their head', to one in which 'the children of the middle and upper classes are beginning to reassert a much older order'.[11] Similarly, music, which from the Beatles and the Stones, through to

Suede, Oasis and Pulp, has often been an expression of working-class artistry, has grown increasingly posh – with the likes of Coldplay, Mumford & Sons and Florence + the Machine coming to the fore. Whilst public-school educated bands like Pink Floyd and Genesis have always existed, it's now the likes of the Arctic Monkeys, who come from working-class backgrounds, who seem like the outliers.

The same applies for top journalists and the commentariat. A report by the Sutton Trust found that around half of the top journalists and commentators were privately educated. The decline of local newspapers and the growth of 'top-down' graduate schemes has largely shut off the non-graduate route in journalism. The background of top journalists doesn't, of course, stop them being able to reflect the concerns and priorities of the bulk of Britain, but the lack of lived experience certainly makes it more difficult. This meant that much of the journalism around the 2016 referendum and 2019 election, with its vox pops and visits to Red Wall seats, felt more like an anthropological road trip than a shared national event. *Moral Maze* and former news presenter Michael Buerk pointed to the danger of this isolation when he argued, 'While we've been worrying about the lack of diverse faces on the screen, or whether women are paid less fabulously than the men, the BBC, and the media generally, have become much less representative of those they serve

– in a more serious way.'[12] A former *Guardian* editor has argued, 'If there are no working-class journalists it would mean that there was no media representation from within a class that, more than any other, requires a voice.'[13] Without more socio-economic diversity, the news media risks continuing to be taken by surprise by events that occur outside a narrow worldview.

The Arts and Humanities Research Council have even gone as far as saying the lack of representation of non-graduate socio-economic groups in cultural occupations represents an 'arts emergency'. They suggest that 'the cultural and creative sector is marked by significant exclusions of those from working-class social origins … The story of social class [within culture] is one of exclusion.'[14] Only 12 per cent of people in publishing or film, TV and radio have working-class origins, and this figure is only 18 per cent for music, performing and visual arts. This has shifted markedly over time. In 1981, only 15 per cent of cultural workers aged under twenty-eight came from upper-middle-class backgrounds, and 22 per cent came from working-class backgrounds. By 2011, this had flipped, with a third coming from upper-middle-class backgrounds and only 13 per cent from working-class origins.

The lack of representation throughout cultural bodies is even more notable at the top, where efforts to highlight diversity in gender and ethnicity have predominated. The

BBC is, of course, the most high-profile example of this. The BBC is one of our great national treasures. Its mission 'to inform, to educate and to entertain' is timeless and the value of public service broadcasting is one that we should cherish and means that the calibre of our broadcasting is so much greater than almost anywhere else. This status as an important national institution, funded by the licence fee, brings with it important responsibilities to represent the whole of the country and to not veer into bias. But in 2017, 25 per cent of the BBC's management team had been to private school, as well as 34 per cent of the BBC leaders who shape BBC news and current affairs coverage. Some 61 per cent of the people who worked for the BBC came from families in which the main earner had a higher managerial and professional job. Even BBC insiders now accept that more needs to be done about this. The new Director-General of the BBC, Tim Davie, was frank about the problem when he admitted: 'There's something about metropolitan-based organisations, or the way you hire, that can somewhat feel a bit distant from some of the population.'[15]

The BBC's head of diversity has said that the Corporation has 'serious issues' with working-class viewers and needs to do more to reconnect to these people. The writer of Radio 4's *Dead Ringers* has acknowledged that many BBC comedians and comedy writers are instinctively anti-Brexit, as it is

associated with conservatism and patriotism and nation-
alism, which are things that comedians generally find
distasteful. I think what some comedians are realising is
that if you are very much London based … that England
and London are two very, very separate places. People in
London should be a little more careful about seeing England as backward and nationalistic or patriotic or racist.[16]

An admission by a BBC writer that most people who
write comedy for the BBC have snobbish attitudes towards working-class people outside London is a pretty
remarkable admission to make. The head of BBC comedy
has even gone as far to say as the BBC represents a 'metropolitan, educated experience', before going on to ask,
'What's the diversity story?'[17] This was clearly noted by
Davie, who acknowledged a metropolitan agenda and
'perceived left-wing bias' in BBC comedy shows. Andrew
Neil went much further when he condemned the BBC's
satirical comedy output, specifically the now cancelled
The Mash Report, as being 'self-satisfied, self-adulatory,
unchallenged left-wing propaganda'.[18]

Although the BBC have rightly acknowledged that
more needs to be done, a very detailed diversity plan announced only a few weeks into the new Director-General's
time in office, which had a large number of detailed met-
rics to allow the BBC to 'rewire' itself in terms of diversity,
failed to mention socio-economic class. At the BBC, along

with other organisations, it's hard to escape the conclusion that although class and education are acknowledged as being important, they fall way behind other 'diversity indicators' in the eyes of decision-makers.

Some argue that this is also reflected in the BBC's news output. It's undoubtedly true that some of the BBC's online reporting and use of social media can betray a liberal, metropolitan worldview, and there's a clear urban and southern tilt. Some reports, such as a particularly one-sided story about Winston Churchill, overstep the mark, but most of the broadcaster's news coverage is resolutely impartial. Roger Mosey, former head of BBC News, has warned that there is an internal battle at the BBC between older journalists, who are strictly committed to impartiality, and younger ones, who want it to become 'more of a campaigning organisation in which journalists shape the agenda to harmonise with their personal views'.[19]

The lack of representation of many working-class areas in newsrooms meant that the Brexit vote of 2016 wasn't properly anticipated prior to the result. Brexit and the collapse of the Red Wall were under-indexed by people who often only heard the views of the London middle class, whereas demand for a second referendum was heavily over-indexed. Former *Today* presenter John Humphrys has argued that this was down to an 'institutional liberal bias' that failed to see the level of concern about issues like Europe.[20] This almost certainly meant that, as well as missing out on the Brexit groundswell in the first place, the BBC didn't note the level of anger at the perception that the vote of working-class people was being ignored. As Mosey commented, BBC journalists shouldn't be expected to agree with Brexit or with Boris-voters from working-class backgrounds, but they 'do need to understand the astonishing range of views in modern Britain and to respect the right to hold them. It is, after all, those people who pay their wages – and if they are patronised or ignored, consent for the licence fee will disappear.'[21]

It's probably little surprise that, in this cultural environment, more working-class people are feeling estranged from one of our most important institutions. According to a poll for the BBC's own annual report, middle-class voters are considerably more likely to feel that the BBC is achieving its mission to 'inform, educate and entertain' than working-class people. Not even half of working-class viewers feel that the BBC 'represents people like them', compared to almost two-thirds of wealthier respondents.

A similar lack of cultural representation at both management and board level is also felt across the cultural sector. As theatre director Javaad Alipoor observes, school boards of governors are almost always more representative than those of cultural bodies. Rather like the political appointments discussed in the Introduction, boards of cultural bodies generally come from a narrow pool of people. Nationally, this generally means well-off, liberal and metropolitan. Such a slim basis often leads boards to panic when pressed by liberal activists, as illustrated by decisions such as the British Library's short-lived attempt to associate Ted Hughes with slavery (because of an ancestor from 400 years ago) and the Rugby Football Union's promise to reconsider the singing of 'Sweet Low, Sweet Chariot'. As Tim Davie acknowledged, a lack of socio-economic diversity matters for reasons of opportunity, but it also matters because it means metropolitan values predominate.

A GULF IN VALUES

At the height of the parliamentary wrangling over Brexit, Jon Snow, the *Channel 4 News* presenter, was presenting the programme in front of a pro-Brexit rally in Parliament Square. Looking exasperated, he announced to camera that he had 'never seen so many white people'.[22] This was odd, given the very white, very middle-class, very Waitrose-picnic-hamper nature of the People's Vote marches. Indeed, a People's Vote marcher even wrote to *The Guardian* that 'I was surrounded almost exclusively by white, liberal, intellectual, middle-class (dare one say it?) *Guardian* readers'.[23] The race of the attendees wasn't really what Snow was getting at, though. Instead, it was almost a dog-whistle to *Channel 4 News*'s metropolitan middle-class, liberal viewers that the demonstrators weren't 'our kind of people' – they were provincial, almost certainly closed-minded, probably less educated and apparently unrepresentative of 'modern Britain'.

Snow and *Channel 4 News* have plenty of form, of course. He reportedly chanted 'f**k the Tories' at the Glastonbury Festival, though he later said he had 'no recollection' of this. The head of *Channel 4 News* described the Prime Minister as a 'known liar'. Cathy Newman saw her interview with Jordan Peterson go 'viral' after her attempt to suggest that the best-selling author was sexist and bigoted backfired.[24] These examples are merely indicative that in the UK what Richard Florida has described as the 'creative class' have values that are very different to much of the rest of the country – and with it they have a pulpit from which to broadcast these values. Florida was clear that his creative class should feel superior to the rest of the population, representing, as he argues they do, 'today's ascending social and economic force'.[25] Much of the creative and media class have a deeply monist worldview and find it incomprehensible that all of their fellow citizens don't share this, meaning that any deviation is put down to stupidity rather than a genuine difference of opinion.

A 2018 report into the lack of socio-economic diversity in culture was stark and honest when it argued that 'cultural workers have attitudes, values and tastes that are very different from the rest of the population'.[26] People who work in culture are highly likely to be middle class, to live, work and socialise amongst the metropolitan 'creative class' and to have liberal political views. They are extremely likely to have voted Remain and to favour an open borders approach to immigration. The creative class represent what David Brooks memorably described as the 'bobos' – bourgeois bohemians – and they generally have views and values to match.

Analysis of the 2020 British Social Attitudes Survey found that on social issues, people who work in culture are the most liberal of all professionals; water and electricity workers were the least liberal. Regarding politics, culture workers are the most left-wing and farmers and finance workers the most right-wing. People who work in cultural jobs are more likely to have a social network that includes people with high-status jobs and less likely to socialise with people who have occupations like bus driver and factory worker.

The homogeneity of the cultural sector might not matter so much if it didn't represent a set of values that, by the nature of the cultural industries, tends to dominate much of national life. Culture isn't only unrepresentative of working-class people; it is also unrepresentative of the views and values of many parts of Britain, including working-class towns, the countryside and parts of business.

IDENTITY POLITICS
– WIDENING THE GULF

Given the already considerable feeling of disengagement from cultural institutions, the decision of these organisations to uncritically embrace some of the most extreme elements of identity politics seems likely to risk even further divergence. As we noted in Chapter Three, identity politics has now become the radicalism of choice for the metropolitan middle class, and nowhere is this as pronounced as in the culture sector. Indeed, the metropolitan creative class have proven to be amongst the most receptive to the message of the activist scholars that we also discussed in Chapter Three. Bobos have pushed hard to use their cultural platforms to pursue an activist form of identity radicalism, which is only deepening the divide between the cultural sector and the rest of the country.

To return to the BBC, the Corporation's strange decision (and then rapid reversal) to allow the playing of 'Land of Hope and Glory' and 'Rule Britannia' but without the words being sung was a judgement that only made sense to the tiny minority of the population who regard these pieces of music as fundamentally racist. *Countryfile*, for example, devoted much of one edition to a report suggesting that the countryside was somehow racist and the beneficiary of white privilege. *Horrible Histories* included a song that was basically an anti-British rant, claiming that 'British things are from abroad, and most are frankly stolen' – a distillation of the desire to denigrate British (and Western history) seen in critical theory.[27] On another programme, a comedian discussed critical race theory before joking about 'killing whitey'.[28] Just as the BBC was pushing the work of its 'gender and identity correspondent', it announced sweeping cutbacks to the local radio and news coverage that had helped it to build links with many working-class communities.

The BBC is by no means the worst offending cultural institution, though. Indeed, the British Library pushed 'wokeness' to an extent that was almost verging on parody. The chief librarian at the library made clear that she felt racism is 'a creation of white people'. She is also part of a 'Decolonising Working Group' at the library, which has discussed declaring a 'racial state of emergency'; replacing 'Eurocentric maps', which are 'tools of power'; reviewing Western classical music because it represents the 'outdated notion of Western civilisation'; and has lamented the battleship design of the library as glorifying racism, as battleships are 'by far the greatest symbol of British imperialism'.[29] In the spirit of the activist scholars, the working group has said that their goal is 'developing and delivering major cultural change'.

Institutions such as the British Museum followed suit, removing the bust of their founder Sir Hans Sloane and adding him to a series of exhibits about the 'exploitative context of the British Empire'. The Arts Council have made clear that they see art as very much a vehicle for political and social change – delivering 'a country transformed by its culture'. The head of the National Gallery has said that it is no longer possible for cultural organisations to 'remain neutral', meaning they now have a role to play in political issues. The Cartoon Museum are 'interrogating their collection' because their 'collection is over-represented with works by white cisgender men'. This, apparently, includes the work of cartoonists such as William Hogarth. The Tate have declared that they have a 'responsibility to act' and even the Science Museum has talked about the need to move beyond 'empty gestures' to 'build on the solid foundation of science capital'. Possibly most perversely, even Kew Gardens joined in the fun, announcing that they would 'move quickly to "decolonise" our collections ... and develop new narratives around them'.[30]

The desire of cultural bodies to be agents of social and political change puts them amongst the 13 per cent of the population defined by More in Common as 'progressive activists'. They are described as a 'vocal group for whom politics is at the core of their identity ... They are politically-engaged, critical, opinionated, frustrated, cosmopolitan and environmentally conscious.'[31] If the culture sector sees itself purely as the voice of the 13 per cent, then it risks cementing the alienation between the creative class and the rest of the country.

TOWARDS A PRO-WORKER CULTURE

The cultural life of the UK has become less about the common good and is alarmingly at risk of becoming a protected citadel for the middle class. Working-class people are less represented in contemporary culture, much less likely to work in the cultural sector or to be represented at its top table and unlikely to see their values represented within the cultural realm. This disconnect has also meant that the cultural sector is often at the front-line of the dismissive snobbery felt by elements of the metropolitan middle class towards less educated voters.

It's clear that such a divide is damaging to both our cultural and national fibre. National culture should not be the product of an isolated, and isolating, separate class that views many of their fellow countrymen with indifference, hostility or disdain. Repairing this divide and creating a cultural life that represents all classes and all of Britain would be an important first step towards repairing our fractured national conversation.

CHAPTER FIVE

WHAT ABOUT THE WORKERS? THE TWO-TIER ECONOMY THAT UNDERPINS THE NEW SNOBBERY

'We don't exist to them do we? Well all of us ****** who don't exist are voting out tomorrow.'

Leave voter, quoted by Dr Lisa McKenzie[1]

'For those stuck at the bottom or struggling to stay afloat, the rhetoric of rising was less a promise than a taunt.'

Michael Sandel[2]

Economic transformation has dramatically decreased the esteem that goes with non-professional jobs, as well as the security and dignity of these positions. Professional jobs, perceived by the economy's 'winners' as being gained through talent and merit, are often seen as the only avenue for success in a modern economy. Celebrating the 'winners' of rapid economic change and depriving many of the 'losers' from a process of dignity, security and respect has meant that many members of the professional class have become disdainful of the views and lifestyles of working-class people.

People aren't just being 'left behind' economically but also in terms of societal esteem, respect and digni-ty. People and places who had suffered from economic change were cast as the authors of their own misfortune, with new jobs having less social esteem than those they had replaced and a politics that spent decades ignoring the concerns of these voters. Decades of being ignored built up understandable resentment. This made the backlash of the Brexit vote inevitable and means that the societal snobbery that has become prevalent since that vote has had an economic foundation. The political and cultural polarisation previously discussed was only made possible by an overweening economic polarisation.

The decline of manufacturing and other structural changes to the economy has led to a situation in which many workers aren't sharing the benefits of growth, and many firms are failing to invest properly in their workforce. Recent decades have created a situation in which many workers are working more but taking home less, as more cash goes to executive salaries, profits and dividends. Economic insecurity has become the norm for many. A belief amongst many London-based decision-makers that aggregate increases in GDP growth are what matters, ignores the fact that, as the saying goes, people don't live their lives in aggregate. The counterpoint to booming cities, and particularly a booming south-east, has been many towns becoming reliant on low-productivity, low-skilled employment that provides workers with little in the way of dignity, security or respect.

This failure has seen the shift from a culture that had reverence for working-class occupations to one that sees 'achievement' merely through attaining professional work. It saw many people in working-class areas move from having economic power, often through mechanisms such as collective bargaining, to becoming economically powerless, and workers moved from having a central to a peripheral part in the social contract.

The winner-takes-all approach has created an economy in which the majority are working harder for less, with work tending to be more insecure and having less dignity. This divide has only been magnified with the Covid-19 pandemic, which meant that the lower-paid faced greater danger and greater hardship.

WHAT ABOUT THE WORKERS? WHO ISN'T THE ECONOMY WORKING FOR?

It is beyond dispute that capitalism is the best way of creating wealth, spurring innovation and growing living standards. For many years, the link between national economic growth, growing productivity and blossoming for individuals throughout society was also clear. Capitalism was not only the best way of creating wealth, but also of ensuring that this wealth could benefit everyone in society: the entrepreneurs with the vision and ideas to build businesses and the workers who played a vital role in creating this wealth. Our economy was able to generate wealth and ensure it was spread throughout society, providing the incentives to help families, communities and society grow stronger and to ensure that all could play an active role in their community. Prosperous and vibrant town centres throughout the country stood as testament to this shared wealth.

The rule was simple: if you worked hard, whether or not you had a university degree, then you would be able to ensure that your family could live in a good manner, get a house, have regular holidays, play an active role in your local community. My grandad, for example, was able to buy a house with a garden for a family of seven on a pitman's wage, and he bought the house from the National Coal Board. My parents were able to buy a house in their twenties. Economic growth was also based on the idea that younger generations would grow up to be better off and more prosperous than their parents' generation. In other words, growth in GDP and productivity would benefit all of society. Such an economy exists as a means to an end – to create greater social cohesion and stronger families and communities – rather than simply an end in itself. At a broader economic level, this grand bargain meant that as the economy grew and productivity increased, so did wages, and this was a pattern that remained intact until the past few decades. Now, the link between national and individual growth appears to be broken.

Measurements such as GDP and GVA are regularly rolled out by commentators, but they mean nothing in isolation. Rising GDP, after all, amounts to little if it isn't felt in people's pay packets and their quality of life. Since 1990, real wages have lagged productivity growth by an average of 0.3 per cent a year, and the gap with median wages has been even greater. In pure monetary terms, if wages had tracked productivity since 1990, the average British worker would be 20 per cent better off. A booming stock market seems like a parallel universe to a worker who barely has time to see their family and has to work multiple shifts with uncertain hours just to make ends meet. Economic insecurity means many families know that they might only be one accident away from economic distress.

The question we should ask is not whether the economy should grow but in what way it can grow and how such growth can contribute towards the common good. How can we ensure that economic growth is not just another meaningless statistic but one in which all are seen as playing a part and in which all are seen as benefiting?

Rebuilding a partnership between workers and businesses in which all sides have rights and obligations is an important way of trying to achieve this.

Sadly, the British economy has not been running to the benefit of workers and the common good for the past few decades. Indeed, we have effectively witnessed a transfer of power and wealth from workers to companies and from the north and the Midlands to London and the south-east. Growth and wellbeing has been restricted to clusters rather than benefiting the whole economy. And this shift in wealth has also included a shift in esteem, with many who have benefited from the transfer of power regarding themselves as uniquely well-suited to making big political decisions. As I set out in *Little Platoons*, there are towns up and down the country that have failed to benefit from decades of economic growth and have seen economic decline along with deteriorating social capital and a brain drain of talented young people.

Plenty have done very well over the past few decades, but this success has been limited to small pools of 'winners', generally professionals based in big cities, and has utterly failed to spread across the whole of society. Most workers, communities and families have missed out on the benefits of a growing economy. GDP and wage growth has also been excessively concentrated in London and the south-east, deepening regional inequalities that continue to blight the economy. Economist Milton Friedman's shareholder value theory continues to dominate in most companies. The theory holds that the primary responsibility of a company is to its shareholders, and the best way of meeting this responsibility is to maximise profit. But this has delivered a short-termist outlook and has detracted from longer-term investment.

It has certainly continued to be a boom time for executives and the financial sector. Executive pay continues to race ahead with no real link to performance. The ratio between CEO pay and the wage of the median worker is now 119:1, and in one firm the CEO earns 1,935 times that of the median worker.[3] This pay gap doubled in the decade to 2008 and has remained stubbornly high since, despite all evidence showing that massively increased CEO pay has had no link at all to company performance. It now takes the average CEO just thirty-four hours to earn what the median British worker earns in a year.

It's also working well for investors. The FTSE 100 more than doubled in value between 2009 and 2019 – but this gain is felt only by a relative few, with share ownership now less than 20 per cent and the proportion of shares owned by individuals halving since the 1980s. In the four years to 2018, the share of profits going to shareholders surged by 56 per cent, whilst wages stagnated and investment in productive activities fell. Property values have also continued to surge, with house prices increasing by over 33 per cent in the past decade. In twenty-five years, the average house price in Westminster has increased twelvefold, compared to a fourfold increase in Consett. Home ownership for young people in their twenties also fell by almost 10 per cent between 2008 and 2018, with a larger and larger proportion having to rent. The decline in home ownership is put into context when considering that, in 1980, the average house price was 5.5 times the average salary; by 1990 it had risen to 6.6 times; now the average house price is almost nine times the average salary. Our modern economy increasingly resembles a capitalism in which fewer people have access to capital.

Corporate profits have continued to rise, reaching an all-time high in the latter half of the Covid-damaged year of 2020. Companies are now stockpiling record reserves of cash and often are failing to invest it productively. The rapid increase (almost a doubling in the past three years) of share buybacks in the UK, where companies repurchase their own shares, risks accelerating the trend away from investment. This represents a further shift from a culture of productive investment to one of circular cash-flows, where the broader workforce are seeing less of the fruits of their labour.

Narrowing the responsibility to shareholders alone means that the social contract by which a company has accountability to its workers, its consumers and the community in which it is based is too often ignored. A key part of the bargain between workers and businesses was once that the worker's loyalty and hard work would combine with the innovation and entrepreneurialism of business leaders to push the business and its profits forward. This partnership also meant that profits would be reinvested in the workforce and spent in ways that made the company stronger in the long term. Now, this social contract seems terribly one-sided, with the bulk of profits being returned to shareholders and executives rather than invested more productively.

A veneer of 'corporate social responsibility' cannot obscure the fact that too much of the modern economy neglects productive investment and has seen the workforce move from being partners in the economy to a secondary consideration. Too little emphasis has been given to the obligation that businesses have beyond those to shareholders. A recent Populus poll illustrated the damage this narrow approach has caused to public trust in capitalism: almost two thirds of people think companies care less about workers now than they did a generation ago, and well over half think that they will care even less in the future. The claim that a rising tide lifts all boats has proven to be trite and flawed.

In the years since the banking crash (which is discussed further later in this chapter) that brought the global economy to its knees, executive salaries have soared, as has the stock market. Until Covid brought on a deep recession, the UK had enjoyed almost a decade of unbroken GDP growth, and unemployment has been low. At the same time, the benefits that should have been flowing from corporate success to the workforce have simply stopped existing for a great swathe of the workforce. For many, the link between hard work and reward seems to have been broken.

Over the same period, 'real wages' – the take-home pay for the majority of working people – had, at best, stagnated. Real wages started to flatten out in the mid-2000s, then plummeted by 13 per cent between the crash and 2012 and fell by around 5 per cent in the decade after. This represents the longest cycle of stagnating incomes since the 1820s. Other than Greece, which saw its economy devastated by austerity and euro membership, the UK has experienced one of the biggest squeezes in real wages of any advanced economy. Recent projections suggest this trend will last until 2025 at least, meaning that the wages of workers have stagnated for the best part of two decades.

This was an acceleration of a decades-long trend whereby wages failed to keep up with GDP growth, employment growth or productivity growth. What economists know as the 'labour share of income' – the proportion of GDP that goes to workers in wages – fell from a high of 65 per cent in the mid-1970s to being stuck in the '50s for the past four decades. For many, this feeling of working harder and harder for less and less reward had become the norm. Part of this ongoing drag on the wages of working people had been caused by a reduction in the bargaining power of labour, but a drag has also happened because wages have simply failed to keep step with the accelerating cost of living and of housing. As alluded to previously, this has also come with a dramatic reduction in the dignity and esteem given to non-professional work.

This story isn't just told by the squeeze in wages and the reduction in the labour share of income but also through a reluctance to invest in the workforce more generally. Research and development (R&D) represents an important indicator of companies investing profits in workers and improved productivity: the UK continues to lag behind other countries. Between 2010 and 2018, the UK's average gross fixed investment was the lowest in the G7. At 1.7 per cent of GDP, our R&D spend is way behind that of South Korea (4.5 per cent), Sweden (3.3 per cent) and Germany (3.1 per cent). We also lag behind France (2.2 per cent) and the EU average of 2 per cent. Our spend has fallen from around 2 per cent in the early 1980s. High-quality R&D is also focused in industries that should be a key to a prosperous future, such as tech and advanced manufacturing. The R&D divide is also a geographical one: R&D per head is over £1,000 in the east of England and less than £300 in both Yorkshire and the north-east. In 2018, the north-east saw only £0.8 billion worth of R&D investment, in contrast to £7 billion in the south-east. This lack of investment has a substantial knock-on impact to output and productivity in the economy as a whole. Even the Bank of England has expressed concern that a myopia based around shareholder value has created a culture of short-termism amongst UK companies, with only around a quarter of British businesses prioritising investment.

Employers are also investing less in training. The Chartered Institute of Personnel and Development has found that, 'despite the central importance of skills development in the workplace, there has been a substantial and long-term decline in the volume of employer training and investment in training in the UK … employers in the UK are training less and investing less in their workforce than they were twenty years ago'.[4] The type and quality of training also seems to have decreased in that time. Between 2005 and 2015, there was a decline of almost a quarter in training investment per employee. This was in contrast to an increase in the EU as a whole of just over 20 per cent. The duration of training fell sharply in the fifteen years from 1997, with the volume of training declining by a half. Adult participation in training generally has also nosedived; over half of unskilled workers say they haven't participated in any training since leaving school, compared to less than a quarter of professionals. Brexit, of course, means that employers might no longer be able to rely on free movement of already trained individuals and will have to think harder about long-term investment in training their workforce.

The pattern over recent decades has become clear, and

it is a pattern that has seen a growing divergence between the performance of the economy as a whole and the economic wellbeing of the workers who fuel this growth. Many companies take a transient and transactional role in their communities, rather than being active corporate citizens. This is representative of the short-term outlook that too much of modern capitalism has. It weakens families and communities and means that the incentives at the heart of the economy have to be fundamentally rethought. Companies should be incentivised to invest in their workers and in long-term innovation, rather than in delivering short-term returns that do little to create a strong and deep economy in the longer term.

Another part of this short-termist pattern, though, is the faith that economic 'winning' is thoroughly deserved and based on talent alone, whereas, conversely, 'losing' is about lack of talent rather than bad fortune. This attitude has been allowed to seep into political and societal attitudes, creating a belief amongst some that the political views of the educated and successful are more valid than the views of the less educated and less economically successful.

THE MERITOCRATIC OBSESSION AND THE GULF IN ESTEEM

A political obsession with meritocracy has dominated British politics since the 1980s. This is the theoretically noble conception that success should depend on merit rather than good fortune. Margaret Thatcher famously said, 'I believe in merit, I belong to meritocracy, and I don't care two hoots what your background is.'[5] Likewise, John Major proclaimed his ambition to build a 'classless' meritocracy in Britain.

Their Labour successors were even more enamoured with the concept than the Thatcherites. Tony Blair peppered his speeches with references to meritocracy, proclaiming that his goal was 'a society based on meritocracy' and only months later boasting that 'the new Britain is a meritocracy'. Blair's meritocracy was 'based on the potential of the many, not the few'. Eleven years later, Gordon Brown said that his ambition was to create a 'genuine meritocracy'. Then, in later governments David Cameron carried on the theme once more for the Conservatives with his 'aspiration nation', which we apparently needed to be to win the so-called 'global race'. Although breaking with much of Cameron's economics, Theresa May maintained the faith in the concept and called for Britain to become a 'great meritocracy'.[6]

If a concept is trumpeted as a good thing by so many Prime Ministers over a period of almost forty years, then it surely is a good thing? Who, after all, could argue with the concept that success should depend on merit rather than accident of birth? The fact that politicians have been proclaiming the meritocratic goal for the best part of half a century suggests that the goal is nowhere close to being achieved. In fact, we saw in Chapter One the domination of the professions by the already wealthy. We also know that those who succeed are particularly keen to ascribe their success to talent rather than chance. Perhaps as important a question is whether the concept of a pure meritocracy creates the conditions and the rationale for the rise of the new snobbery.

Indeed, the downside of pure meritocracy was clear to the man who came up with the phrase. Michael Young was a remarkable polymath. He drafted large parts of Labour's extraordinary 1945 manifesto and established both the Consumers' Association (now largely known as Which?) and the Open University, but he is probably now best remembered for writing *The Rise of Meritocracy*. Rather than advocating for the merit-based system, Young's goal was to write a darkly dystopian fantasy that warned of the dangers of a society that had meritocracy as its organising principle. In Young's meritocracy, success was dictated by the formula 'IQ + talent = merit'.

In this imagining, society divides into two classes: the eminent and the remainder. The successful would marry other successful people until the meritocracy became a self-contained, self-perpetuating and dynastic class of its own, in which 'nearly all parents are going to try to gain unfair advantages for their offspring'. In this society, 'the eminent know that success is a just reward for their own capacity, their own efforts'. And those that haven't risen to the top 'are tested again and again ... If they have been labelled "dunce" repeatedly they cannot any longer pretend; their image of themselves is more nearly a true, unflattering reflection.'[7]

This goes hand in hand with the reduction in esteem for less-skilled occupations in recent years, as well as the changing nature of those jobs themselves. Working-class jobs used to be secure and an important source of pride, meaning and identity. This esteem wasn't just felt by people working in these jobs but also by society as a whole. Now, many jobs at the bottom of the skills ladder are deeply unfulfilling, insecure and a source of neither pride nor identity. They don't generate esteem either for those working in such precarious circumstances or for much of the rest of society. The sense of being at the bottom of the pecking order with high levels of insecurity might also contribute to mental health issues associated with diminished esteem, with lower-paid workers significantly more likely to demonstrate mental health problems.[8] The inevitable stresses that come with struggles to make ends meet, combined with diminished social status, reduced family time and a meritocratic concept that low status equals low talent, might all contribute to this diminished sense of personal esteem. Journalist James Bloodworth correctly observes that 'Britain today resembles Young's dystopia only in the sense that disproportionate rewards are showered on the elite and contempt is increasingly shown to those at the bottom'.[9] Without an attempt to raise the esteem of work that is currently low skilled and low paid, societal divisions will only continue to fester.

In his book *The Tyranny of Merit*, Michael Sandel sums up the impact of a meritocratic society on esteem when he observes: 'For those who can't find work or make ends meet, it is hard to escape the demoralizing thought that their failure might be their own doing, that they simply lack the drive and talent to succeed.'[10] Hayek, who thought rewards should depend on market value rather than perceived merit, was also quick to see the potential downside of a culture that lionised merit. He saw that

a society in which it was generally presumed that a high income was proof of merit and a low income of a lack of it ... would probably be much more unbearable to the unsuccessful ones than one in which it was frankly recognised that there was no necessary connection between merit and success.[11]

Both Hayek and Young were able to see the impact on esteem and status of a myopic approach to meritocracy. If those at the top were there purely on merit, surely the same applies to those at the bottom, with all of the implications on status and esteem that come from that. The political pushback of Brexit and the 2019 election was also in many ways a revolt against an economic culture that applauded the successful and ignored those in low-skilled work. Redressing the balance should be an important task for the post-Brexit generation, armed with the tools of greater economic autonomy provided by leaving the EU.

Young lived until 2002 and felt that he saw the future he worried about becoming a reality. He suggested that 'education has put its seal of approval on a minority ... and its seal of disapproval on the many who fail to shine'.[12] Shortly before his death, he talked about his prediction of the elite 'becoming less and less concerned with the main body of people, establishing a sort of culture of their own, an elite culture with a good deal of arrogance in it. These things have largely happened.'[13] As Patrick Deneen has commented, 'The economic and social order increasingly rewarded the "able" and abandoned any commitments to shoring up the conditions of the meritocratic losers ... The material as well as psychological inequalities inescapably arising from the new system undermined its legitimacy.'[14] Stagnating incomes, greater insecurity, reduced esteem and poorer health outcomes all stand as testament to the material and psychological inequalities that Deneen points out.

An economic culture purely formed on the basis of meritocracy is one in which an insidious form of snobbery can take hold. Such a culture persuades the wealthy and successful that they have achieved their wealth and success purely because of their own talents, and as Sandel puts it, this creates a culture of hubris at the top and humiliation at the bottom. Indeed, LSE research has shown that the most successful are the most likely to agree that economic disparities are based on disparity of talent. A culture of meritocracy taken to its extreme can create a belief that only the views of the successful should count.

The developments that we have discussed in this book, in which middle-class political activists have seen fit to denounce working-class people as 'stupid and bigoted' and metropolitan comedians have made working-class Brexit supporters the butt of their jokes, is one legitimised by a system that argues society has been sorted based on 'merit'. In tandem with excess deindustrialisation, it has helped to create a gulf in esteem and dignity, which has relegated the concerns of workers to beneath those of the managerial class.

MORE PEOPLE LIKE US? THE PHILOSOPHY OF ESCAPE AND WHY SOCIAL MOBILITY ALONE ISN'T ENOUGH

The twin to meritocracy is social mobility, which has become an article of faith amongst much of the political and economic class. In many ways, it's a deeply laudable aspiration, tackling the issue this book has considered that many of our professions are deeply unrepresentative of the population and that young people from working-class backgrounds are seldom seen in these jobs. What Sandel calls the 'rhetoric of rising' has dominated the politics around social mobility over this time; the concept that the gifted should be able to 'rise as far as their effort and talents will take them'.[15] This is attached to a concept that the economy will reward hard work and effort, which, as we have seen, is often not the case.

The problem comes when social mobility becomes the catch-all project of social reform or, for some politicians, the only project of meaningful social reform. David Cameron, Nick Clegg and Tony Blair were all particularly fond of talking about social mobility during an era that valorised higher education, professional jobs and social mobility and diminished vocational education, manufacturing and those 'left behind'.

When many members of the political or managerial class talk about social mobility, they are saying that their goal is to enable a handful of people from working-class backgrounds to become 'people like us'. Used in such a way, social mobility doesn't become a tool of social progress; rather it becomes an ideology of escape, where the talented few can leave their hometowns and become part of the gilded elite. There is an underlying assumption that professional or managerial jobs, based in cities, are the only possible, and certainly the only desirable, choice for

young people with talent, and an underlying lack of com-
prehension about why anybody would want to pursue a
different route.

I was most struck by this concept about a decade ago,
when I edited a collection of essays from MPs who had
come from working-class backgrounds. They all had impressive life stories, with many coming from the humblest
backgrounds to become Conservative MPs, and often
having successful professional careers on the way. The
moral of most of the stories was the same: if you work
hard and are determined enough then you too can be a
success. The tale, as with many social mobility success
stories, was of glass ceilings smashed, multiple career suc-
cesses achieved and this success allowing people to leave
their humble origins behind.

Nick Timothy recalls a similar tale of former Education
Secretary Justine Greening talking about how hard work
had allowed her to get out of her hometown of Rotherham and pursue a successful career in London. She wrote:
'All the years I spent growing up in Rotherham, I was
aiming for something better ... an interesting career, a life
that I found challenging.'[16] In all cases, success is defined
as 'getting out' and pursuing a professional career. Unwit-
tingly, then, an emphasis on social mobility has placed
the emphasis on success and escape for the few with too
little weight on what this means for the less determined,
less academically gifted or, simply, less lucky. The story of

social mobility is written by those who wanted to 'get out' rather than those who wanted to stay.

At its best, a project of social mobility is essential to ensuring that our professions are open to the most talented people, rather than being a closed shop. At its worst, social mobility becomes a chimeric goal, with a focus on a fortunate few and no acknowledgement of the structural issues of an economy that remains tilted and two-tiered. A myopic social mobility discourse actually plays a part in the culture that underpins the new snobbery, with some members of the professional class arguing that the only means of achieving fulfilment is by gaining a professional job, and the only way of gaining this professional job lies in getting 'up and out' of a struggling hometown. In other words, membership of the professional class should be expanded slightly, and little or no thought should be given to those left behind. Combined with a fetishisation of meritocracy, it creates a psychological culture where it is acceptable to give the talented an opportunity to escape, with those not sufficiently capable having to stay behind in an environment of insecurity and decaying high streets.

The only social mobility story is an upward one – of young people from poorer backgrounds using their talents to become a part of the emerging professional elite. It is never a two-way street; children from the professional elite are expected to remain a part of that elite, with a small number of young people from poorer backgrounds being enabled to join them. The rhetoric of social mobility is not that of the son of a city banker becoming a factory worker.

As is a familiar story throughout this book, the decline of manufacturing that was most acute in the UK created a two-tier economy which maintained that success could only be achieved in professional and managerial jobs. It is this mantra that then led to a severe gulf of esteem between those professional jobs and others. The almost uniquely geographical centralisation of the UK economy in London (as well as a handful of professional jobs in other major cities like Manchester) also created the growing geographical division we have seen, with successful people from provincial towns effectively encouraged to leave (and possibly never return to) already struggling towns and strengthen an already vibrant metropolis. The people and places left behind have had to deal with economic decline and an increasingly decayed public realm. Hence, social mobility without creating more high-quality, fulfilling jobs throughout the economy risks widening disparities of esteem and creating a gulf of understanding. Social mobility is important, but social mobility alone is not enough.

THE DECLINE OF SKILLED WORK

Throughout much of the twentieth century, working-class occupations were viewed with real reverence throughout society. There was pride that Britain led the world across several industries, and pride in the people who worked in them. Working men and women were seen as heroic figures, crucial to British economic and military success. My hometown of Consett was famous for producing the steel that made our battleships and nuclear submarines, and the metal that built great structures across the Empire. There's still pride that this small north-eastern town could create so many things of such significance, and I'm still extremely proud that my grandad was a foreman fitter – a skilled and important role in a steelworks that had many skilled and important jobs.

My other grandad worked as a pitman in the Durham and Northumberland coalfield. It was a dirty and dangerous job (he died young and died a miner's death of black lung), but again there was pride and community spirit attached to the work. The 'aristocrats of the working class' were well paid for their work, both because it was dangerous and (before the unpardonable folly of Scargillism)* because they were organised. Conditions in these dangerous industries – especially mining – had also improved

---

* The Miners' Strike of 1984–85 has been romanticised as a great last stand for a way of life, but Scargillism, with its belief that a strike should be imposed on a membership (with a ballot frequently being denied), its overtly political desire to supplant domestic authority and its frequent rejection of potential settlements, meant that the damage caused to British industry and mining communities was even greater than it otherwise would have been. The way the mines were closed, and the social and economic damage that caused, was unforgivably harsh, but the stance of Scargill, using the future of an industry and communities as a political pawn, made the situation even worse.

as people understood the significance of the jobs to the country, respected and revered the work being done and appreciated the importance of work being done with dignity, in decent conditions. As such, from the sweeping social reforms of Disraeli's government onwards, the mission of successive governments became, in Disraeli's words, 'reduction of their hours of labour' and to 'humanise their toil'.[17] Labour was gradually dignified, the esteem given to manual work was felt throughout society and workers were treated with genuine respect.

Miners Hall in Durham stands as an architecturally impressive testament to the former power and status of coal mining and manufacturing. Chamberlain Square in Birmingham is a reminder of the grandeur that came with manufacturing and the ability of manufacturing to catapult somebody – in this case Joseph Chamberlain, one-time manufacturer of screws – to great political power. Herbert Morrison's famous rejection of Britain playing a role in the embryonic European Union (a rejection shared by most of the giants of that monumental government) on the grounds that the 'Durham miners wouldn't wear it' stands as a reminder of the political power of manufacturing.[18]

The fact that a town 'made' something and was famous for making something gave real pride to the people who worked in manufacturing, and to everyone who lived in that town. That kind of pride can't come from call centres or distribution hubs; pride and rootedness doesn't come from towns becoming dormitories for nearby cities. Connection with a manufacturing base emphasised dignity and skill and also provided employment that went well through the supply chain and well beyond the site of the industry itself. This helps explain the sheer economic and social devastation that followed the closure of industry in places like Consett. Paul Kennedy, the award-winning historian and author of *The Rise and Fall of the Great Powers*, remembers the importance of industry to creating a sense of community when he grew up in Wallsend. He recalls:

> There was a deep satisfaction about making things. A deep satisfaction among all of those that had supplied the services, whether it was the local bankers with credit; whether it was the local design firms. When a ship was launched at [Newcastle firm] Swan Hunter all the kids at the local school went to see the thing our fathers had put together ... this notion of an integrated, productive community was quite astonishing.[19]

This community spirit wasn't just found in the industrial pride but also in the neighbourhood institutions that industry brought with it. In Consett, for example, the steelworks paid for the local cricket and football teams, worked with the local technical college and had a huge number of social clubs, including the Steel Club that still takes pride of place in the town centre. As I've discussed on many occasions, the decline of social capital and community spirit is something that should concern us all, and at least part of that decline in community has to be associated with the decline of industry and of dignified work.

The descendants of the Durham miners don't have the same political or economic status as their ancestors; the reverence for workers that previously existed has been replaced by the newly fashionable snobbery. Since the 1970s, the UK has deindustrialised more than any other major economy, from around a third of the economy to only 10 per cent. This was done in the name of modernisation, with an assumption that manufacturing could be 'outsourced' as the UK would otherwise become too expensive to compete. It has meant that we spent years betting the farm on services, finance and the 'knowledge economy'. These sectors are all important, but this focus has resulted in 'success' being concentrated in a graduate-heavy knowledge economy, clustered in cities, with high-status and generally lucrative jobs. At the other end of the economy, the skilled manufacturing jobs that once dominated have been replaced with relatively low-skilled, insecure, low-paid jobs. Whereas esteem used to be spread evenly across the economy, it is now reserved for jobs towards the knowledge end of the economy. The aftermath of deindustrialisation has created an economic polarisation, which has led to a political polarisation and a growing gulf in understanding and empathy.

A good job in manufacturing used to provide secure work, a decent wage and pride that a worker was doing an important job, as part of a company that they felt emotionally attached to and which played a key role in the national economy. These companies brought respect and a sense of place to towns. The decline of manufacturing changed the nature and shape of British society and has been devastating to working people and communities. It has been a major cause of most of the trends considered in this book, of societal divides and declining worth. Above all else, it has created work without meaning and work without dignity.

This has combined with a rolling back of the gains in working conditions and a diminution in the bargaining power of labour versus capital. Working-class jobs have less esteem, fewer rights, less security and fewer avenues for progression than was the case many years ago. As alluded to earlier, in many towns, the great industrial giants of the past have been replaced with call centres, distribution hubs and a number of other jobs where there is precious little dignity and precious little community pride. Many jobs are low paid and precarious, with over three-quarters of all workers feeling more anxiety and insecurity in their work than they did a generation ago.

James Bloodworth has told of how many workers in distribution centres are treated with utmost suspicion, are given tags to monitor their movement and are reluctant to even have toilet breaks for fear of missing their 'targets'. Almost 4 million workers in the UK are in insecure jobs, meaning they mightn't even be aware whether they are working until the day itself. In many workplaces, the worker's voice is now non-existent.

What was sold as modernisation and a focus on a 'knowledge economy' too often resulted in public decay and low-paid, precarious, insecure work. This was starkly illustrated in a survey of workers who had been laid off by the Rover plant in Longbridge in 2005. Although 90 per cent of workers gained another job, the average wage for these workers was almost £6,000 a year less than it had been at Rover. This is a clear illustration of the fact that all jobs are not created equal. Although many who lost their jobs following deindustrialisation were able to find other work, this new work was often lower paid, with less security and less social esteem than the skilled manufacturing job they had held before.

It wasn't just the post-industrial towns that took the hit from the UK's rapid deindustrialisation; it was the economy as a whole. One of our major national problems is the fact that our productivity lags behind most major European countries, and low productivity means we are generating less wealth as a country. Productivity is also lower outside the south-east, meaning 'the regions' are falling further behind. The sector that drives productivity growth more than any other is manufacturing – just the sector that successive governments were happy to allow to wither. UK manufacturing productivity is 12 per cent higher than any other sector, and up to half of the productivity growth since 1997 in regions like the north-west and the Midlands has come from manufacturing.

This is not to romanticise the past. As I made clear in *Little Platoons*, the industrial work that kept many communities alive in the past was often dangerous and stressful. It also meant that many women were locked out of the workforce. But that was an argument for modernisation within manufacturing, rather than modernisation without manufacturing; the assumption underlying this economic shift was wrong. Any argument that deindustrialisation was inevitable is deeply flawed and ignores that sector's success in other countries.

Treating deindustrialisation as an unalterable economic inevitability or a sign of progress and 'modernisation' was mindless at best and negligent at worst. Manufacturing decline has left our country poorer, less productive and more economically divided. It has also meant that too many parts of the country have become long forgotten, too many workers stuck in insecure work and too many high-status individuals feeling disdain for and disengagement from their fellow citizens.

COVID – SHINING A LIGHT
ON THE TWO-TIER ECONOMY

Many communities that were once dependent on skilled, proud work found that they were buffeted by two major economic shocks in a matter of decades. The first, de-industrialisation, saw massive economic dislocation, widespread unemployment, greater insecurity and, ultimately, greater dependence on both unskilled work and the public sector. Decades later, the highest levels of 'worklessness' were in those places that were most reliant on heavy industry. Just as many of these places had started to recover from the first hammer blow, the banking crash delivered another hit.

The sight of people queuing outside Northern Rock in anticipation of the first run on a British bank since the 1930s was particularly devastating because it happened outside a financial establishment that had gone from a respected and solid local institution and lender to north-eastern industry to one that had gambled so recklessly they literally bet the bank and lost. The deepest recession since the Great Depression, started by the irresponsible behaviour of bankers, ultimately inflicted the deepest damage on those communities and those people that had borne the brunt of previous downturns. Whilst finance pretty much carried on as before, the public realm in many already struggling communities decayed further.

The damage caused by the austerity that followed the bankers' folly could be seen in high streets and shared spaces across the country. The Centre for Cities found that the five places hardest hit by public spending cuts were Barnsley, Wakefield, Doncaster, Liverpool and Blackburn. Whereas London and the south-east had recovered to 2008 GDP levels within months of the crash, it took areas like the north-east the best part of a decade to recover. The think tank Onward has also found that the fraying of the social fabric was greatest in those areas that had faced economic dislocation. When the time came for left-behind places to answer how they felt about decades of economic neglect, they seized the opportunity. Nobody should have been surprised when all but one of the former coalfields voted for Brexit.

Twelve years after the banking crash came another catastrophe that hit hardest those communities who were suffering the most from over a decade of stagnating real wages. With over 100,000 deaths, Covid-19 was devastating for the entire country, but the lower down the income scale you were, the worse hit you were by both the economic and the health impacts of Covid. Put simply, it's easier to work from home in most middle-class jobs than in most working-class jobs, and social distancing was simply not an option in many unskilled positions. One study found that those with household incomes of over £50,000 a year were six times more likely to be able to work from home than those whose household income was less than £20,000. According to the ONS, the mortality rate in the most deprived areas was two and a half times that in the least deprived areas.

Plenty of non-graduate jobs at the lower end of the income scale also brought with them more risk and exposure, both in the job itself and in travelling to and from work using public transport. Images of Tube trains packed with workers before dawn caused concern but emphasised the grim fact that many low-paid workers had to risk their health during the pandemic because they simply had no other choice. The fact that supermarket workers were 75 per cent more likely to develop Covid than the population as a whole was a grim illustration of the risks taken by many low-paid workers. The characterisation of the necessary lockdown being a phase where 'middle-class people hid while working-class people brought them things' might have been simplistic but was certainly not without a kernel of truth.[20]

The greater exposure to the virus also meant that those at the bottom of the skills ladder were the most exposed to the risks of the pandemic. The *British Medical Journal*, for example, found that amongst working-age people 'men working in the lowest skilled occupations ... had the highest rates of death from Covid-19' and the ONS concluded that 'men working in elementary occupations had the highest rate of death'.[21] Those industries in which lower-paid, less-skilled workers tended to cluster, such as hospitality and retail, were also amongst the hardest hit economically, whereas sectors such as finance were able to carry on much as before.

More than any previous economic crisis, the Covid pandemic has made crystal clear the disparity in worth applied to different jobs within the economy. By shining a light on the issue, though, it also emphasises to the entire nation that some lower-paid workers might be 'invisible', but they have been essential at keeping the country and the economy moving during this incredibly difficult time. The weekly applause for NHS workers was a crucial part of this national sense of appreciation, but the work of supermarket workers, transport workers, delivery workers, care home staff, security guards, construction workers and others who had to put themselves in danger was also increasingly recognised as essential and valuable. The next step is to ensure this sense of appreciation becomes a belief that everyone is entitled to dignity and security at work.

SUCK IT UP? THE MYTH OF INEVITABILITY

Generations of politicians, economists and commentators saw these profound economic changes as somehow inevitable, positing that political actors were powerless to do anything about the overwhelming forces of change.

Thatcher's dictum that 'you can't buck the market'[22] was willingly embraced by politicians of left and right, eager to accept a new paradigm in which the economic and political disarmament of the state was taken as a simple and unavoidable fact.

In the United States, Bill Clinton put it most starkly when he claimed that 'change is upon us. We can do nothing about that.' If anything, Tony Blair, Clinton's 'Third Way' twin, took the powerlessness even further when he argued that 'you might as well debate whether autumn should follow summer.'[23] For Blair, this new world that he celebrated was one in which countries should compete to 'attract capital as it moves'. It was 'indifferent to tradition. Unforgiving of frailty. No respecter of past reputations. It has no custom and practice.' It probably says something about Blair's skills as an orator (as well as how the Labour Party had changed) that this paean to the inevitability of economic dislocation caused by footloose capital was given at a Labour Party conference and gained a rapturous standing ovation.

As with their ideas about meritocracy, Blair's successors shared his inherent belief that the economic status quo represented the unchangeable natural order of things. Gordon Brown celebrated the fact that financial services represent a 'larger share of our economy than they are in any other major economy', boasted of his 'light touch' approach to financial regulation and, a year before the financial crash, trumpeted that a 'golden age for the City of London' meant that 'a new world order was created'.[24] David Cameron saw the bloated nature of the City of London as a 'great British success story' and was happy that the economic 'debate is now settled', with all 'candidates for high office' having to sign up to the same orthodoxy.[25]

That orthodoxy was that the nature of the global economy was as much an act of nature as the sun rising in the morning; that this economy was based on self-correcting markets, financial services and a knowledge economy; and that the only choice was to adapt to this new reality or perish. It was accepted that the new economic order was non-negotiable and that rather than harking back to a golden age of unionised heavy industry, the UK should be focusing on its 'comparative advantage' in finance and in services.

At the same time, a cult of competitiveness developed, with the maxim being that the UK should ignore manufacturing and ensure its people could be 'competitive' in the new economy. The resulting financialisation of the UK economy led to the hollowing out of much of the real economy and to the situation where, as Pope Francis suggests, 'finance overwhelms the real economy'.[26] The growth of financial services began in the 1980s, when investment in the financial sector increased by 320 per cent compared to only 12 per cent for industry, and has been maintained ever since. This financialisation coincided with a deep and damaging deindustrialisation, which transformed the UK from a production-led to a consumption-led economy. An equally important transformation was the financial sector moving from one that existed to provide capital for productive investment in the real economy to one that predominantly existed as an end in itself to provide rapid speculative returns. Financialisation has also drained talent from the productive economy, accelerated regional inequality and, as we've seen, left many politicians unable to contemplate an alternative.

An increased pooling of economic benefits, a stagnation of real wages and a hollowing out of working-class towns were all regarded as part of this inevitability. The new political economy did not consider how to ensure that this new economy worked in the interests of the people, nor did politicians consider how the rougher edges of the new settlement could be dulled to minimise the impact on workers. Instead, the message was that working people should suck it up; change was inevitable. The only way out was for people stuck in decaying towns to educate themselves in order to compete in the knowledge economy.

Politicians like Gordon Brown grew drunk on the possibility of what this new, unchallengeable reality might bring, predicting in 2007 that 'by 2020 we will need only 600,000' unskilled jobs.[27] As predictions go, this wasn't one that should have Mystic Meg quaking in her shoes. When 2020 came, there were as many as 13 million unskilled jobs, and 9 million of these were insecure. The knowledge economy was important, but not as important as the bold predictions suggested, meaning that graduates, as well as many non-graduates, were becoming stuck.

It was, of course, all based on what might be charitably described as a misunderstanding. The decline of many parts of the economy, and with it societal esteem for many workers, was not inevitable. The hollowing out of manufacturing, the dependence on finance and services, the stagnation of wages and the reduction in esteem for the jobs done by most of the population were not, after all, forces of nature. Instead, it was the product of poor decision-making and a lack of national ambition. They were political choices, and to choose another path will also be a political choice. Mrs Thatcher denounced industrial policy whilst actively pursuing one to build up the City of London and make the UK a home for finance. Successive governments made the political choice to let the UK deindustrialise more than any other major economy and, with it, lose much of the legacy of skilled engineering and skilled work that had made the country prosperous. For decades, politicians made the conscious decision that stagnation in 'left-behind' towns was unimportant because GDP as a whole was increasing. Similarly, the political decision was made to focus completely on academic education and reduce the funding, resources and importance of skill and technical education.

Other countries did not think industrial decline in advanced economies was inevitable and haven't seen the consequent reduction in esteem for workers. Manufacturing represents a quarter of output in Germany, almost a third in South Korea and only 10 per cent in the United Kingdom. This has had the knock-on effect of making the UK less prosperous, less productive and its economy less balanced. All of this is based on politicians believing in the inevitability of economic change and rendering themselves powerless in the process.

The certainty of each generation being better off than the previous one has also reached a shuddering halt. The Institute for Fiscal Studies has found that those born in the 1980s 'have income that is no higher in their early thirties than those born ten years before – and this is the first time since (at least) the Second World War that that has happened'.[28] For many young people, the push towards a university education and professional work has merely left them with a trail of debt, lost work experience and no 'graduate premium' in earnings. Onward has found that for up to a quarter of graduates, this earnings premium simply doesn't exist partially because, as Goodhart and others have observed, we over-estimated the potential size of the knowledge economy and ultimately left a hefty proportion of young people in limbo.

The inevitability paradigm that is dominating debate today is around automation of the economy, with some spuriously arguing that AI-driven automation will make job losses inevitable. As Oren Cass argues in his excellent *The Once and Future Worker*, such predictions miss the fundamental point and assume a continuous and steady state. Automation if used ambitiously will not destroy jobs but will improve output and prosperity, which represent the key to increased wages and better opportunities. Rather than assume inevitable decline, we should be considering how an ambitious, pro-worker industrial policy can result in change for the better.

TOWARDS A PRO-WORKER ECONOMICS

Recent decades have seen the common good relegated as the benefits of economic growth have been felt by a small number of people. Many workers have been running just to stand still, seeing their wages stagnating, their leisure hours decreasing and their life becoming less dignified and more precarious. The political economy of this change has settled into a deeply insufficient dichotomy of government-led redistribution on one side and escape for the few through social mobility on the other. We should be asking how we can create an economy in which all workers have dignity and respect, and in which all jobs allow workers to support a family and play an active role in community life. A tilted, two-tiered economy must be one that works to the benefit of all in society, rather than one that only benefits the high-status elite and with it makes the new snobbery economically institutionalised.

An economy should provide the incentives that encourage the innovation that creates wealth, improves our lives and makes us all richer – but the conversation shouldn't end there. If the economy isn't providing dignified, esteemed work to everybody in a way that strengthens society as a whole, then we should consider how it can better work for the good of everyone. This aim should be the North Star of a pro-worker approach to economics.

CHAPTER SIX

BEYOND THE SECESSION
OF THE SUCCESSFUL

*'It is the fault of too many to mistake the echo of a London
coffee house for the voice of the kingdom.'*

Jonathan Swift[1]

Deborah Mattinson, one of Britain's leading opinion pollsters, spent years in the so-called Red Wall seats in the north and the Midlands in the run-up to and aftermath of the 2019 election. Her focus groups and interviews uncovered the same level of pride in the industrial pasts of many towns that I feel about Consett. Just as Consett is proud that it produced the steel that built bridges and structures across the Empire and made naval ships and British submarines, so Accrington, for example, is proud of producing the NORI bricks that built the Empire State Building. Steel from Consett, bricks from Accrington, pottery from Stoke-on-Trent – all towns that were defined by the industries that have now largely been obliterated.

Mattinson noted how throughout her conversations people complained about nothing replacing the industries that had been lost, with these voters feeling 'left out', ignored, looked down upon and told what to think. She recalled that every time she recounted her findings on Twitter, she was met with a barrage of angry responses all saying something along the lines of 'We don't care what these idiots think.'[2]

People feel looked down on because they have been looked down on. The concerns of these working-class voters have been neglected and ignored for decades. A decline in admiration for the work that many non-university graduates do has been accompanied by a decline in the respect given generally to people from working-class towns. As previously discussed, the political prescription to solving the problems faced by working-class Britain has all too often amounted to helping a small minority to leave the working class, with little thought given to those left behind. This is no longer nearly good enough. We should accept that many people don't want to leave the place in which they grew up, nor want to leave their families and communities behind, and that all should be able to have a sense of dignity, esteem and social standing in what they do.

A gradual societal separation, with two parts of the country having different working, sporting, eating, educational and shopping experiences, has effectively meant that parts of the elite have begun to live separate lives from great swathes of working Britain. Whereas a large part of the post-war period was one in which working-class life and occupations were greatly respected, many low-paid occupations are now almost forgotten and ignored.

Elements of this elite have adopted a mono-worldview, which brings with it a sense that 'all sensible people' must share that view and a belief that all those outside those opinions are worthy only of contempt. Economic and social liberalism has maintained a grip, with a belief in open borders, free flows of capital and trade, and has condemned anyone who disagrees as being driven by a closed mindset towards a closed society. In doing so, many have eschewed the democratic, the national and the local in favour of the technocratic and the transnational. Even the common understanding that comes with patriotism and a shared sense of common endeavour has, for some 'social justice warriors', been overtaken by a narrow sense of identity politics, which serves only to diminish common threads and deliberately sow division.

The coalition of the economically prosperous is keen to point to the dangers of 'unfiltered' democracy in an 'increasingly complex world', with this complexity seemingly best understood by the wealthy and successful. As such, the elite reaction to the EU referendum result came from the same elite belief that it was an example of ordinary people being given power over an issue that they cannot understand. A deviation from the status quo thus came to be seen as democratic hysteria, or what Nye Bevan would have described as an 'emotional spasm', rather than what it was: a logical and thought-out democratic choice.

Whilst the elite has become more powerful and more cut off from the rest of society, it has also increasingly put up the 'no entry' signs. A 2011 BBC survey found that members of the elite were twelve times more likely to come from the most privileged backgrounds than they were to come from a working-class background. Doors are opened by connections and 'networks' and closed to all but a handful of outsiders. It's little wonder that a former Conservative Prime Minister said it was 'truly shocking' that 'in every single sphere of British influence, the upper echelons of power are held overwhelmingly by the privately educated or the affluent middle class'.[3] The perception of a detached and largely closed elite, with a tin ear to the concerns of those outside the circle of the successful, was undoubtedly a major factor in the ground-swell of anger that led to the vote to leave the EU.

When the likes of Robert Reich and Christopher Lasch developed the concept of the 'revolt of the elites' and the 'secession of the successful' in the late '80s and early '90s, even they might have been how surprised at how quickly the prediction became a reality and its staggering impact on the politics and economics. Lasch argued that elites had increasingly abandoned the middle class and the poor and that politics had lost moral values, and Reich claimed that the successful were becoming deliberately disconnected from their fellow citizens. Such a 'secession of the successful' has resulted in some opting out of the bonds of solidarity and mutual respect that are crucial to maintaining a healthy and well-functioning democracy. Many of these winners from economic dislocation and change feel themselves a natural part of what Jefferson described as a 'natural aristocracy' based on 'talent and virtue', with this perceived talent allowing them to look down on the less fortunate, who are regarded as deserving of their fate. The 'winners' tend to agree with Locke's societal division between the 'industrious and rational' and the 'quarrelsome and contentious', with both sides seeing the other as problematic. Modern society might have seen an elite sorting into an aristocracy, but it is much more likely to be based on birth than talent or virtue. Equally, Locke's concept that both sides see each other as problematic is clearly seen when one side derides less educated citizens as bigots and gammons and people in forgotten communities increasingly push back against a mindset that has left their communities ignored. Sneering from the successful can only lead to the build-up of resentment amongst those being sneered at, with ongoing political repercussions.

For many, economic stagnation and a decaying public realm came to be seen as an acceptable price to pay for a moderately growing aggregate GDP, the benefits of which are felt much too thinly. As such, the disillusion, despair and disempowerment felt by many long-ignored communities was heard loud and clear in the Brexit referendum in 2016. These same communities also made quite clear how angry they were at a political elite that openly called for this verdict to be overturned. Working Britain made it quite obvious in 2019 that they believed their verdict should be respected, and that they were prepared to abandon generations of anti-Toryism on the promise of improved lives, better jobs and more dynamic local economies. That promise must still be delivered.

COVID-19 – A CALL TO ACTION

Our national experience during the Covid-19 pandemic has made the necessity for the promised change even more urgent. The pandemic has clearly shone a light on the tilted nature of the economy, and as we have previously discussed, the lowest paid have been more exposed to both the health and financial risks of the virus. Lockdowns have meant that high-income earners have built up savings, whereas those on lower incomes have seen savings disappear and debt grow. The fact that people working in elementary jobs were more than twice as likely to die of Covid was a stark reminder that the UK's economic divides aren't merely theoretical.

The pandemic has been a pivotal time for the UK, and we must learn its lessons in order to reboot how our economy and society works. It has served as a wake-up call, and the importance of manufacturing has been quite clear, with its role in producing PPE, ventilators, testing kits and vaccines. In a crisis, countries simply need a strong domestic manufacturing sector or face grim consequences. The Covid crisis also laid bare how the political choices made to diminish the role of manufacturing have left the country exposed. A lack of manufacturing capacity meant that the UK initially faced a shortage of key equipment when the pandemic first hit. The reality of closed borders caused by the crisis, combined with the need to ensure supply-chain resilience in the future, emphasised the importance of reversing the decline of our industries.

Covid has, however, also illustrated that the UK has considerable strengths. Building on these strengths could undoubtedly create a stronger future. The first asset has been a restoration of many community bonds and at times a feeling of national solidarity. During lockdown, many people spent considerably more time in their local community as workplaces closed; the weekly applause for key workers brought neighbours together in support and appreciation of many important workers; the importance of high-quality shared community space, community facilities and community businesses became more important. In doing so, Covid might have revived the importance of neighbourhood solidarity and provided the basis for the rebuilding of community infrastructure after the pandemic.

The UK's remarkable achievement in rolling out the most successful vaccine programme of any large country is also a reminder of the success that can be achieved when government, business and world-class researchers work together towards a key strategic outcome. Britain's formidable research base was able to develop a vaccine remarkably quickly, and government supported this effort and also ensured that there was sufficient manufacturing capacity within the UK. The existence of a company like AstraZeneca within the UK was also crucial and provided an advantage that would have been lost if Pfizer's proposed takeover of AstraZeneca (which was passionately supported by market fundamentalists) had gone through in 2014. The vaccine success is a reminder that industrial policy really works when it is done right and focused, laser-like, on strategic priorities. This lesson of calculated focus and strong manufacturing is something that we must maintain post-pandemic, and with it help to build millions of secure, well-paid jobs that could help to revive long-forgotten parts of the country.

PERMANENT REALIGNMENT. A MULTI-RACIAL, WORKING-CLASS, ONE NATION SETTLEMENT

The left's pursuit of a narrow identity politics and consequent abandonment of great swathes of the working class opened the door to political realignment, which concluded in the dramatic toppling of the Red Wall in 2019. Whilst Brexit was one element of this switch, the fact that voters felt belittled, patronised, ignored and lectured by parts of the modern left was another important factor.

The biggest Tory majority for four decades gives the government the political capital to deliver substantial and lasting economic change. The trust being placed in a once hated Conservative Party is a trust based on a desire for economic transformation and an improved quality of life. It is a trust placed by voters who had never voted Tory before and wouldn't have even contemplated doing so as little as a decade ago. One former Cabinet minister observed that he'd never heard about as many 'grandparents spinning in their graves' as he had during the election campaign. Voting Tory was an important psychological moment for many of these voters, and it involved coming to terms with historical incidents where the party was seen as 'the enemy', moving loyalty from a Labour Party that was once seen as a part of working-class identity. As Labour peer Lord Glasman has argued, victory was achieved by 'transforming the class basis of the Conservative Party'.[4] Maintaining this transformation is crucial.

'Get Brexit Done' was a compelling message to voters who had long been ignored and who were determined not to have their vote disregarded again. But it is not a message that can be of electoral relevance now that Brexit has actually been done. To shift Red Wallers from 'lending their vote' to a more lasting move means aligning Tory priorities absolutely with those of the working class. Dignified work and safe, strong communities which are great places to live and bring up a family must be a key part of this. A permanent realignment can happen by relentlessly focusing on the working-class voters who delivered a Tory majority.

These voters made a brave and often tough decision because of the shift on the left and a promise of positive change to their lives, local economies and communities. The government must ensure that the next few years deliver profound economic change to long-forgotten parts of the country and in doing so provide economic security, dignity and respect.

For many years, the priorities of the economy and politics have been tilted in favour of graduates, professionals and the south-east. Restoring the balance, focusing on the needs of the 'lagging regions' and creating a vibrant future should be crucial. Successfully achieving this would deliver a permanent and lasting realignment, whilst the left becomes lost in the maelstrom of identity wokeness. This change can only be brought about by always asking which policies can deliver an improved standard of life for the long-forgotten voters; if the interests of city-based Tory donors and working-class voters clash, it should always be the interests of the working-class voters that win out. In the words of Winston Churchill, now is the time to make 'finance less proud and industry more content'. Infrastructure spending should be prioritised in those parts of the country that have been long neglected.

The issues that we have addressed in this book make it clear that four decades of myopic liberalism have failed great swathes of Britain, leaving our industry weaker, communities more scattered and the country more divided. It cannot be true that a bigger dose of the ultra-liberalism that caused the disease could represent the cure. Instead, we must focus on building a country that unleashes the entrepreneurialism and invention that creates wealth but also creates institutions of dignity, community and mutual respect.

This goal of providing economic security and esteem should be the cornerstone of an appeal that is properly multi-racial and working class. It would, in the finest spirit of that phrase, be a One Nation settlement that strengthens families and communities, ensuring no part of the country is left behind and all citizens can share in growing prosperity.

One Nation Conservatism has for too long just been seen as an extension of 'liberal conservatism' or even (and ludicrously) as the Tory branch of the pro-EU movement. In contrast, genuine One Nation is a reaction to the excesses of economic liberalism. Disraeli set out his objections to liberalism in a way that seems oddly prescient given the divisions the country faces today:

> Liberal opinions are the opinions of those who would be free from certain constraints and regulations, from a certain dependence and duty which are deemed necessary for the general and popular welfare. Liberal opinions are very convenient opinions for the rich and the powerful. They ensure enjoyment and are opposed to self-sacrifice.[5]

He worried that whilst 'immense fortunes were accumulating ... the working classes, the creators of wealth, were steeped in the most abject poverty'. The One Nation Conservatism of Disraeli and Macmillan is the one that is most relevant today – a belief that dogma is wrong, that economic growth must be shared and that no communities or regions should be left behind.

Similarly, the conservative Labourism that flowed from the chapels and trade unions through to the building of New Jerusalem also has a crucial role to play. Long forgotten in a left obsessed with identity, it is the belief in a society defined by patriotism, mutual obligations and strong communities. It's hard to imagine a modern Labour leader uttering the words that Clement Attlee spoke in 1950 when he defined his vision of

> a society of free men and women – free from poverty, free from fear, able to develop to the full their faculties in co-operation with their fellows, everyone giving and having the opportunity to give service to the community ... a society bound together by rights and obligations, rights bringing obligations, obligations fulfilled bringing rights; a society free from gross inequalities and yet not regimented nor uniform.[6]

Attlee's concept of rights and obligations is an important one as we look to develop a partnership between workers and business, with business having a right to make a profit but also an obligation to invest in their workforce.*

It was Robert Kennedy who best articulated the hopes for a society that emphasises dignity rather than aggregate measures like GDP, when he recalled seeing

---

* The tradition of Catholic social teaching, with its belief in the common good, should also be considered more deeply as we look to restore dignity and pride to lives. Catholic social teaching holds that 'economic growth will not be limited to satisfying men's needs, but it will also promote their dignity'. Pope Leo XIII summed up what should be the underpinning of a renewed economic settlement when he said that workers 'who contribute so largely to the community may themselves share in the benefits which they create'.

proud men in the hills of Appalachia, who wish only to work in dignity, but they cannot, for their jobs are gone and no one – neither industry, nor labor, nor government – has cared enough to help … Even if we act to erase material poverty, there is another greater task, it is to confront the poverty of satisfaction – purpose and dignity.[7]

Although this speech was made over fifty years ago about a different country, it is still oddly relevant to the UK today. The men in the hills of Appalachia, who have seen their jobs disappear with nothing being done to help, could equally be in the post-industrial towns throughout Britain, who saw their concerns waved away by generations of politicians. The diminution of dignity and respect is clearly also a theme, which we have addressed a number of times in this book.

Building an enduring economic settlement would be of far more value to the country than becoming stuck in the endless trenches of a culture war. The priority must be to build genuine social solidarity through economic reform, in contrast to the identity-obsessed social justice warriors of the new left, who want to see society as perpetually divided based on group identity. It is essential that we focus on the real problems faced by BAME citizens, such as high unemployment faced by black men, health inequalities and excessive use of stop-and-search, but don't let an obsession with identity-focused division further damage national solidarity, nor get in the way of measures that will improve the quality of life for all workers. The words of Martin Luther King Jr, that people should be judged by the content of their character not the colour of their skin, should again inspire us more towards the goal of an equal society.

People from an ethnic-minority background, for example, are much more likely to be stuck in low-paid work. Tackling the economic insecurity faced by low-paid workers and taking steps to strengthen community and family life will do more to change lives than a million well-meaning social media posts and endless discussions about statues, street names or microaggressions. A media circus about avant-garde theories or the politics of Churchill might help to boost the media presence of previously obscure academics, but it won't improve the quality of life for black Britons; it will distract energy from tackling deep-seated issues in criminal justice, the economy and healthcare.

By becoming intoxicated by a narrow identity liberalism, the modern left has detached itself from the everyday concerns of working people. In doing so, it has relegated the concerns of workers to the periphery and opened the door to a lasting realignment. Some on the right are also not innocent bystanders in this debate. In a desperate desire to start a 'culture war' for political advantage, they risk entrenching the divisions that are being fuelled by the left. Rejecting the divisive politics of the identitarians and being proud of our country and its history doesn't mean that we should ignore the underlying issues faced by many ethnic minority Britons. Instead, it means we should re-double our efforts to tackle these issues.

Above all, we should remember the fact that people, regardless of gender, sexual preference or race, are proud of being British, proud of our history and want a better life for themselves and their families. We should be proud that, as Trevor Phillips points out, the UK has more ethnic minority politicians in senior government positions than the entire EU. Whilst a small minority look to fight a culture war, we should aim squarely to ensure that workers, whatever their identity, are able to live and work in dignity and respect.

The new settlement this book calls for is based on a multi-racial conservatism, improving quality and dignity of work for all, tackling injustices where they exist and enabling everyone to live a more fulfilling life with their family and community. A multi-racial, pro-worker politics focusing on decent money and dignified work will do more to improve the quality of life for all citizens than Instagram posts by middle-class radicals or cliché-ridden interventions from wealthy celebrities. A new economic settlement needs to reject the identity-obsessed radicalism of the rich in favour of an economic and political settlement that is relentlessly empowering and relentlessly pro-worker.

RESTORING DIGNITY, ESTEEM AND POWER: TEN STEPS TO BUILDING A PRO-WORKER SETTLEMENT

The new snobbery has proven to be more enduring, more mainstream and more socially acceptable than the old, which makes it all the more insidious. Mainstream elite conversation all too often doubts the ability of working people to make complex democratic decisions and can adopt a sneering tone towards occupation, education and accents.

A gradual coming apart of a real sense of solidarity has combined with a decades-long reduction in power, esteem and dignity for large parts of working Britain. Many workers have been robbed of their pride, respect and security by economic changes, and too many people from low-income backgrounds continue to be left behind by the education system. Just as financialisation has left finance unmoored from the real economy, too many members of the elite feel detached and apart from the sense of national solidarity that a democracy needs to thrive.

For many at the other end of the economy in Britain today, work isn't just shorn of respect; it also prevents them from playing a fuller role in family and community life. For too long, it's been expected that if you don't pursue a professional career, you would have to 'make do' with an income that stagnates at best; a town and public space with an all too visible sense of decay; and a feeling of disdain from some of your fellow countrymen. That must change. Escape mustn't be the only route to success, and 'mobility' shouldn't only be leaving your town but also being able to get a decent, skilled job in your hometown. Millions of working people should no longer be peripheral to the national story nor regarded as legitimate objects for scorn from those with a habit of 'punching down'.

Brexit provides us with the opportunity and, crucially, the levers and tools to restore this power, dignity and respect. We have the chance of pursuing a different path, and one that will make a real difference to people's lives. The government's goals of 'levelling up' and pursuing a 'net-zero' economy should be rocket boosted with a tightly focused and ambitious industrial policy that aims at remaking the economy. This would include restoring dignity and status to working-class occupations, with a clear aim of creating millions of skilled, secure jobs in manufacturing. Education should be reformed so it delivers for and empowers all citizens, not just the academically gifted. Power should be transferred to working people in the economy, in their communities and in those institutions that have long ignored the concerns of working people.

This programme for a new, pro-worker settlement has at its heart the need for economic and cultural security. For many people, security is far more important than Westminster Village terms like inequality (which can be seen as academic and most think doesn't relate to them) or aspiration (which is difficult when people are only just managing). Providing workers with economic security is a crucial element to achieving stronger families and stronger communities, but so is ensuring that people don't feel buffeted by constant change. We shouldn't be afraid to celebrate continuity, the familiar and the local, and to emphasise building relationships and remoralising the public realm.

A national renewal should be founded on economic ambition for a national capitalism that is based on productive manufacturing and which rebuilds the productive partnership between businesses, communities and workers. A manufacturing that restores a sense of pride in work and pride in place should be allied with an attempt to use manufacturing to drive the UK towards being the first net-zero-emissions economy. Such a renewal would ensure that all in society can have pride in where they work and their engagement in the workplace; pride in where they live; and pride in their contribution to the local community.

A ten-pronged approach towards a new pro-worker settlement can restore the balance in politics, economics and culture and move working people from the periphery to the centre. Overriding all of this should be a clarity that snobbery based on socio-economic factors is unacceptable. The ugly caricaturing of parts of Britain as ignorant, bigoted, feckless or lazy has become socially acceptable in too many circles and should be no more acceptable than other forms of prejudice.

Each of these ten concepts identified in the approach represents a power shift towards working people:

1. Prioritising government spending on those areas in need of an uplift and placing the resources of Whitehall at the service of local communities.
2. Strengthening representation of working people in the political class, in business and in cultural bodies.
3. Placing the creation of millions of high-quality manufacturing jobs at the centre of our economic goals.
4. Ensuring that government protects early-stage innovation and incentivises innovation in post-industrial areas.
5. Making growth in median wages a core economic goal.

6. Developing a network of strong and area-limited local banks.

7. Repairing the dignity of work.

8. Deepening the partnership between workers and businesses and institutionalising it in corporate governance.

9. Putting vocation and skill at the heart of our education system.

10. Building strong and active communities.

1. Prioritising Government Spending on Those Areas in Need of an Uplift and Placing the Resources of Whitehall at the Service of Local Communities

A new economic settlement, harnessed within a strategy of levelling up and having the industrial capacity to be a global leader in advanced manufacturing, as well as the pursuit of a net-zero economy, should run through everything the government does, with the resources and the cohesive vision to go with it.

Running through the new economic settlement should be an approach to the state and to public spending that sees money diverted to those areas that need it the most, meaning that Whitehall exists to serve local communities, rather than the other way round. For years, infrastructure investment has been excessively focused on already successful regions, and this has also included public spending on areas such as R&D, meaning that existing regional inequalities have been reinforced. Rather than attempting to run the economy from Whitehall, it should be the role of government to provide the right infrastructure and the right incentives to enable economic growth and a strong private sector in those parts of the country that have been struggling for too long.

When considering infrastructure spend, it is essential that government considers how to prioritise lagging areas, so their relative lack of infrastructure doesn't become a reason for these places to fall further behind. Emphasis should be placed on those areas that need infrastructure spending the most. Broadband is one such example, with research by the Centre for Towns showing that cities have almost 40 per cent faster broadband speed than small towns. Levelling up should mean efforts are made to ensure the right digital and transport infrastructure is in place to encourage companies to locate in and people to move to post-industrial towns. Although major transport programmes will take some time, emphasis can be placed on things that will make a difference in the interim, such as radically improving the local bus network.

2. Strengthening Representation of Working People in the Political Class, in Business and in Cultural Bodies

Building greater national solidarity means building a country where the views of working people are represented across institutions, rather than being ignored or sidelined. Ensuring that business, culture and politics have baked-in working-class representation will be an important step. This would make an important contrast to the status quo, where working people are numerically excluded in many key institutions – from the House of Lords to the patchwork of government agencies – which risk becoming elite talking shops aiming to perpetuate a minoritarian worldview.

Part of the drive to improve representation comes from the need to rethink the concept of diversity. Diversity consultants are keen to emphasise the importance of this as widely as possible, but few extend the concept to achieving socio-economic diversity. When the concept is raised, the authors of books populated with impenetrable jargon and monist certainties tend to inform us that socio-economic factors are too complicated. That is, of course, humbug and reflects the truth that an emphasis on class would demand more self-sacrifice and self-reflection than the existing narrative creates room for. As Walter Benn Michaels recognised in his brilliant *The Trouble with Diversity*, an obsession with cultural and identity differences has meant that discrepancies of wealth and class have been ignored, leading to a 'vision of social justice that delivers us nothing'.[1]

The first step to improving representation clearly lies in politics. Whilst diversity in politics has improved in recent years regarding LGBT, ethnic minority and female MPs, it has regressed when it comes to class, with 85 per cent of MPs being graduates. This extends far beyond the green benches and into the wider political class. Making a push to have more working-class representation in Westminster is essential to having a politics that leaves fewer people disengaged and is genuinely representative of working Britain. Just as parties successfully, and correctly, pushed to increase the diversity of Parliament in other ways (often with the support of impressive groups such as Women to Win), they must now see it as a priority to increase socio-economic diversity. The House of Lords also represents an avenue for increased representation. The Lords remains a hermetically sealed institution of south-eastern, elite opinion – it's probably unsurprising that it opposed Brexit at every turn. A reform of the Lords that increased regional representation would be a substantial improvement.

Of course, the political class doesn't begin and end in the Houses of Parliament. The non-departmental bodies that have a considerable influence on how policy is made and how it is implemented are often full of the great and the good, with both the regions' and the workers' interests not sufficiently represented. It means that although the views of Red Wall voters have increased in importance since 2016, their voices are still not heard in many of the committee rooms (or Zoom calls) where key decisions are made.

The last Labour government introduced an Equalities

Act, which had nine 'protected characteristics' that had to be considered when making public appointments – but it neglected to include socio-economic factors, including occupation variety. This meant the government took its eye off the ball when it came to socio-economic diversity, at a time when working-class Britain was already feeling ignored and under-represented. Government should consider socio-economic and regional diversity when making appointments to non-governmental groups and should also develop innovative ways of connecting with disengaged communities. This should also extend to other public bodies that have an important institutional focus within communities, such as the magistracy and bodies like school boards of governors. We might look to replicate the model by which Go-Ahead bus group encouraged its drivers to become magistrates. Having greater working-class representation within the political class is essential to having a politics that consistently reflects the needs and priorities for all of society.

Politics is not the only profession where people from working-class backgrounds are underrepresented at all levels. The cultural industries in particular are increasingly middle class at all levels, with much cultural output seemingly written by the middle class for the middle class, with the aim of mocking the views and lifestyles of the less successful. Familiar surnames dominate all elements of cultural industries, from newspaper columnists to fashion, with what Julie Burchill described as the 'SADs' – the sons and daughters of the rich and famous – building up a new cultural aristocracy. As discussed earlier in this book, the BBC, a great national institution, possibly represents the most concerning example of a cultural institution that has been captured by what its new Director-General described as a southern, metropolitan mindset. Only recently the BBC published detailed analysis of its various diversity targets, but its main comment about socio-economic diversity was that it is 'a relatively new area of best practice'.[2]

Again, the notion of diversity in the entire cultural sector is narrow and largely ignores socio-economic class. This has the result of leaving great swathes of the population feeling excluded. Cultural institutions becoming 'less metropolitan' must move beyond rhetoric and be reflected from board level down. Cultural bodies should look to ensure that internships (which must be paid) and other devices that have been used to reward connections and networks should instead be focused on improving chances for groups that have been shut out. In order to become less metropolitan, the cultural sector must develop mechanisms, such as bursaries, to reach out to parts of Britain that they've long forgotten. And those cultural bodies that receive taxpayers' cash should be expected to illustrate continual improvement in this field or face having taxpayer subsidies reduced. Having more hubs in post-industrial towns could also be a way of ensuring that a greater diversity of life experience is reflected in our culture.

The former head of the government's Social Mobility Taskforce didn't hold back when he described many professions as a 'closed shop' that depended on 'birth not worth' for entry and advancement.[3] Despite this, many parts of the business world still haven't taken sufficient steps to show they are taking socio-economic diversity seriously, with class taking a back seat to identity-led diversity. Too much of the debate is also focused on an elite level – as many column inches are devoted to the need for diversity on FTSE 100 boards as they are at broadening the basis of firms more generally. Having more diverse firms from entry level up is crucial to changing corporate culture.

It's essential that big business begins to show that it is taking diversity of economic and class background seriously. Boosting employment of women, LGBT and BAME people is important, but employing more black people from working-class backgrounds is very different to employing more BAME Etonians. Large businesses, who are already expected to file a gender pay gap report annually, should also be expected to report on how they are increasing socio-economic diversity. They should consider increasing the proportion of entry-level jobs offered to non-graduates and also changing recruitment practices

to adopt methods such as the 'CV free' recruitment utilised by the likes of *The Spectator*. As we'll discuss later,
worker representation must also extend beyond greater
socio-economic diversity in the workplace to worker
representation on company boards and remuneration
committees.

3. Placing the Creation of Millions of High-Quality Manu-facturing Jobs at the Centre of Our Economic Goals

It is essential that we remake the economy so deindustrialisation is replaced by rapid reindustrialisation. An
industrial policy with an explicit goal of increasing the
manufacturing share of output is essential to boost productivity, revive long-suffering towns, ensure economic
resilience and build a high-skill, high-growth, high-wage
economy.

If there was a single event that illustrated the division
of British society in the 1980s, and with it the retreat from
heavy industry towards a 'service-led economy', it was
the Battle of Orgreave – a grim and violent clash between
miners and the police. Alastair Stewart said the so-called
battle was a 'defining and ghastly moment in a period
of turmoil that split the United Kingdom and changed,
forever, the conduct of industrial relations and how this
country functions as an economy and as a democracy'.[4]
It was grimly symbolic of failed industrial relations, a
union movement that had been quick to choose militant

madness and a governing elite that had lost ambition or strategy for industry.

Four decades on from that bloody and awful day (for which South Yorkshire Police and the National Union of Mineworkers leadership both still have questions to answer), Orgreave is now home to a Composites Technology Centre for McLaren Automotive. Other parts of the north that were once symbols of industrial greatness and industrial decline also offer glimmers of hope of industrial revival. Blyth, which suffered the double blow of the decline of its pits and the decline of its ports, now has the promise of a 'gigaplant' for electric car batteries. Probably the best example is the Nissan car plant in Sunderland, which is now one of the most productive car plants in Europe.

The McLaren factory in Orgreave is also a reminder that the UK is very, very good at both high-level manufacturing and inventing things. Most Formula One teams are based in the UK, and we are rightly renowned for our ability at innovation, with a long-standing inability to convert our brilliance at innovation to brilliance in developing British companies that 'monetise' that innovation. In short, we have long been much better at the research than the development or commercialisation side of the equation.

The major challenge is to shift from a country that is renowned for inventing things to one that is also renowned for making things, and in doing so create millions of secure, fulfilling jobs that allow for more dignified work and stronger families and communities. Sadly, stories of manufacturing success are all too often the exceptions that prove the rule of lasting deindustrialisation – and this wasn't just a 1980s story; the UK has also deindustrialised more than any other major economy *since* 1990.

Many things were lost in the decision made by successive governments to shift the UK from being a major manufacturing nation to one that relies on services. For many years, parts of the libertarian right spread the gospel that the UK had little future in manufacturing and that we should instead make the most of our 'comparative advantage' and become a service- and finance-led economy. They also argued that, with a bit of guidance from the government, the market would turn around those towns that could no longer rely on manufacturing. Manufacturing's share of output fell from almost 30 per cent in 1970 to around a third of that level today, with closure rather than modernisation chosen for many elements of the British manufacturing industry. The service-led nirvana that some promised turned out to be one that transformed dignified, trained work to low-skilled, low-paid, low-security work for many.

A revival of manufacturing and an explicit aim of re-industrialisation could also bring about the revival of many parts of the country that have long been declining, with cutting edge industries helping to provide meaning and develop a sense of belonging and local pride. The creation of millions of skilled jobs that bring dignity, pride and fulfilment could help transform the financial landscape and remake the economy in a way that benefits local areas but also the economy as a whole.

Manufacturing is generally higher skill, more productive and more export-driven than other sectors. Whilst it accounts for less than 8 per cent of jobs in the UK, it accounts for around two thirds of our R&D investment – the kind of investment that is crucial to future growth and prosperity. This R&D emphasis also underlines the importance of manufacturing in creating what Willy Shih and Gary Pisano have described as the 'industrial commons' – skills and knowledge networks and clusters that drive innovation further.

We must pursue an active and intelligent industrial policy, with a clear goal of reindustrialisation. Brexit, and in particular not being subject to the EU's restrictive state aid rules, gives us much more flexibility to do this. A post-Brexit, post-pandemic reset provides a springboard for us to deliver that altered economic settlement and to pursue a bold strategy that focuses on a high-tech, green reindustrialisation of our economy.

To reindustrialise also means reckoning with the mistakes of the past. It should be targeted at those post-industrial towns with manufacturing heritage and pride that continues to blossom and shine through. We should also be prepared to learn from the economies that have created a much more balanced system, and particularly those in Asia, which have focused on key sectors. Comparatively, past efforts at UK industrial policy seemed to create a 'sector deal' for everybody without much targeting whatsoever.

Taiwan, for example, saw a decline in manufacturing but has since successfully reindustrialised, with manufacturing increasing from a quarter of GDP in 2009 to around a third today. The countries that saw the biggest sustained growth not driven by natural resources were the Asian Tigers, notably Taiwan and Korea. As the IMF has noted: 'The success of the Asian Miracles cannot be disentangled from that of their industrial policies.'[5]

South Korea also saw manufacturing-inspired strong growth from the 1960s onwards, and the industry continues to contribute well over a quarter of GDP. In 1961, the North Korean economy was a third bigger than the South Korean economy; now South Korea's GDP is fifty-four times bigger than its communist neighbour. The industrial policy that allowed South Korea to enjoy decades of 'hypergrowth' and real wage growth of almost 20 per cent a year was predicated on favouring 'positive-sum entrepreneurship', defined as activities that benefit the wider economy and boost productive capacity – as opposed to 'zero-sum entrepreneurship', which represents short-term speculation and rent-seeking. Korea is also taking the lead in utilising technology in manufacturing, with over 800 robots per 10,000 workers, compared to 300 in Germany and eighty-five in the UK. This use of technology is enabling an increase in output with no net hit on jobs, with a recent European Commission paper finding that 'robot adoption tends to be positively associated with aggregate employment'.[6]

For the Asian Tigers, government was able to utilise a sensible industrial strategy that used market signals to direct resources and protect early-stage innovation. They have been rewarded with strong economic growth, rising real wages and GDP per head and have also proved much more resilient during the Covid pandemic. We should learn from these lessons as we look to create more dignified, skilled jobs.

Even the IMF, which spent years preaching the benefits of unhindered markets and little to no government intervention has had to accept the importance of industrial policy in the rise of Asia. In 2019, they acknowledged that 'the success of the Asian Miracles was not a matter of luck but the result of [industrial policy]'. The 'strong commonalities' of the policies pursued by the Asian Tigers included the 'preeminent role of industrial policy in their development', which has meant their 'economic model resulted in much lower market income inequality than in most advanced countries'.[7]

The successful industrial policies utilised by the Tigers

are deeply different from those the UK adopted in the 1970s, which gave the policies a bad name. Whereas the British strategies of the 1970s focused on propping up existing industries and import substitution, the Asian Tigers have spent a relentless focus on being ahead of the curve for the industries of the future. Indeed, the likes of Korea were highly active in terms of patents granted from an early stage in their industrial policy development. As such, the Tigers placed a real emphasis on innovation and export as part of their push.

The role of government within industrial policy is in supporting the supply of factors of production (such as skills, which should be done through proper technical education) and key industries and technologies. The job of government shouldn't be to pick particular firms and products but to support development in those industries that the market suggests are likely to be important in the future, and in which the UK could be at the cutting edge. At this stage in industrial development, the state has an important role in fixing market failures that prevent the UK playing a key part in emerging industries, and steering capital and labour towards these industries. As the IMF argue, 'By intervening to fix market failures to develop sophisticated sectors and domestic or homegrown technology, the state could create conditions for high and sustained long-term growth.'[8]

This industrial policy shouldn't be about bucking the

market but instead using market signals about emerging technologies to maximise the impact of state investment. In these Asian examples, the feedback mechanism of the market allowed governments to identify sectors for future growth and provide investment – enabling these countries to be leaders in key sectors. This is just the approach we should use towards advanced manufacturing, and in particular towards green manufacturing, with the goal of making post-industrial England the global leader in low-carbon, net-zero manufacturing industries. Government is uniquely placed to use this feedback mechanism to invest, as well as ensuring that infrastructure and finance are in place for the strategic sectors in which the country could lead and prosper.

This should also involve a targeted strategy that builds on measures announced in the 2021 Budget and uses mechanisms such as tax breaks and capital allowances to make companies more likely to invest in capital equipment. These tax breaks should be greater for manufacturing businesses and particularly beneficial for net-zero manufacturing based in post-industrial areas. In other words, government should maximise tax breaks and incentives for investment in key strategic industries in those parts of the country in need of revival. These decisions should be made based on market signals, rather than the whims of policy-makers. And a focus on export and relentless competition between companies in key emerging sectors should also be an important part of any emerging industrial policy.

Asia was able to learn the lessons of industrialisation and industrial policies in the West. Now we can return the favour and learn lessons from Asia to deliver a targeted industrial policy that puts the UK at the forefront of emerging industries, strongly pushes productive investment and revives long-declining parts of the country.

4. Ensuring that Government Protects Early-Stage Innovation and Incentivises Innovation in Post-Industrial Areas

An ambitious industrial policy should be supported by a determination to maintain British companies in key strategic sectors and to help innovative British companies to scale up rather than sell out. What has been described as the 'valley of death' between research and commercial viability should be bridged over by government support for innovation and invention.

Many of those post-industrial areas that are most in need of revival have fuelled the kind of innovation that changed the world in the past, and they can do so again. George Stephenson's remarkable inventions in the north-east of England helped to power the Industrial Revolution. Joseph Swan developed the prototype of the incandescent light bulb in 1860, almost two decades before Edison patented his. Gladstone Adams even invented the windscreen wiper after being caught in snowy weather on the way back from a football match. Such a spirit of invention should be harnessed today as part of an ambitious industrial policy that aims not only to encourage innovation in the UK but also to ensure that this invention is commercialised by British firms. We must be clear with our goal to be the most innovative country in the world, with both overall and public R&D spending that is greater than the OECD average and puts us ahead of countries such as Germany, who currently spend 3.1 per cent of GDP on R&D, compared to our 1.7 per cent.

A model should be developed that explicitly protects invention and innovation and directs this towards post-industrial areas. In the mid-twentieth century, the United States, inspired by Vannevar Bush through the Defense Advanced Research Projects Agency and the National Science Foundation, used such a strategy to boost American competitiveness and deliver the decades of rising living standards the country experienced until the 1970s. Such a strategy involves government investing in and incubating innovation and helping to transfer ideas from the initial invention to the marketplace. This links national strategic priorities with the benefits of new business ideas and protects and nurtures early-stage innovation which is both fragile and risky.

This model, in which the government nurtures invention at the most important stage and invests in those companies at the cutting edge of key emerging technologies, could be transformational for the UK economy, which already has a world-leading research base but often lacks the ability or the means to push that into the marketplace. A network of innovation hubs based in post-industrial towns could bring together business, academia and government to ensure that innovation happens in the UK, is commercialised by UK firms and benefits the areas that need it the most.

An effective industrial policy could maximise the UK's strengths and use the directional sway of government to promote long-term growth outside the south-east. We should also follow the example of the Asian Tigers and have a powerful investment board, with fiscal powers to encourage investment in post-industrial areas.

A targeted and coherent industrial policy aimed at re-industrialisation would help to restore skilled, dignified jobs that workers and communities can be proud of. It would help to restore prosperity to areas that have been declining for decades, as well as boosting wages, productivity and balanced growth. Crucially, rather than simply looking to rebuild the industries of the past, it would also give once declining parts of the country a leadership role in industries of the future and help the UK to become a global leader in delivering green manufacturing and the first in the world to deliver a net-zero-emissions economy. Industries such as next-generation solar power and the production of electric batteries for non-petrol cars should be a crucial part of our emerging economy. They also produce the kind of jobs that revive a sense of place and pride and narrow the economic divides that have played such a role in creating a deeper national rift.

The Covid crisis, and in particular the role of Astra-Zeneca, has also taught us a salutary lesson about the importance of having domestic companies in important strategic industries and not leaving our national resilience and supply chains to the whim of hedge funds and asset strippers. The success of the vaccine scheme in the UK, following earlier mishaps around protective equipment and testing, has shown that it is a national imperative to have British representation in the strategic industries that are important to us and will be essential to our future. Combining this realisation with an attempt to revive post-industrial towns could be utterly transformative.

5. Making Growth in Median Wages a Core Economic Goal
For many years, wages have been seen as a secondary goal in economic policy. Major financial news is often accompanied by images of the stock exchange or by reports of market moves, and inflation and the level of the deficit are obsessed about by commentators, just as the Balance of Payments (BOP) was in the 1950s and 1960s.

The economic trend that explains recent years more than anything else isn't the stock market, the BOP or even unemployment. Stagnating real incomes for the majority of workers has, more than almost anything else, contributed to political disengagement and the rise in populism. Even with that realisation, median wages tend to be relegated to the secondary basket as economic indicators. Despite this, there is no better indication of whether an economy is working for the majority of people. As such, median wage growth should be a primary economic indicator and a primary policy goal. *The Economist*, once the house journal of neo-liberalism, recognised the need for this shift in April 2021, when it argued, 'It is right to judge economic progress by the purchasing power of median wages, not profits or share prices.'[9]

The minimum wage and national living wage have been important policies in reducing very low pay, but there is clearly more work to be done. Continuing with sensible increases in the living wage should continue to be an economic priority, as should altering the 'taper' element of universal credit so that people are able to take home more of their pay. Ensuring that large firms in particular are returning more profits to workers, rather than shareholders or executives, is an essential way of making sure the economy benefits all those who work in it. Taking home increased pay doesn't just restore the link between a hard day's work and a fair day's pay; it also enables workers to spend more time with their families and in their local communities. Increased median wages as a core economic goal will be beneficial to society as a whole.

6. Developing a Network of Strong and Area-Limited Local Banks

A network of regional and local banks, with government support and the support of the existing banking sector, would also provide a longer-term, more local supply of capital in parts of the country that have long been dependent on the short-termist financial sector. The decline of building societies and the rise of a centralised financialisation meant that the City of London became stronger; post-industrial towns lost assets and access to finance; and the economy became more short-termist and focused on the whims of the financial sector. A network of local banks, only allowed to lend in their local area and encouraged to lend to manufacturing in particular, would be a key way of decentralising finance. If it was funded by a levy on those banks that benefited from the bank bailout, it would also represent the kind of change that should have been achieved after 2008.

The sheer dominance of the City of London has created a drain of talent towards the capital, but it has also meant that the City is 'the only game in town' when it comes to finance. The decline of local sources of finance, including building societies in particular, meant manufacturing faced an uphill battle to gain finance for longer-term projects, and small, innovative companies had difficulty securing the funds needed to 'scale up'.

Such a change would be of more than symbolic importance. First, it would contribute funding for the kind of high-quality skilled work that would help to transform local economies. Second, it would allow lending decisions to be made by people with a real understanding of the needs of the local area, rather than by a desiccated London-based banker or an even more desiccated algorithm. Third, it would allow local banks to play a fully active role in their local and regional communities. Rather than national banks using a fig leaf of a 'corporate social responsibility', regional and local banks could be fully engaged in communities that they are actually a part of and help to provide the finance and support that these communities need.

7. Repairing the Dignity of Work

The building of a strong, vibrant economy in those places that have long been left behind was what so many voted for when they protested against the existing economic settlement in 2016, and when they broke with generational voting habits in 2019. This requires reindustrialisation, strategic government investment, town centre revival and, just as importantly, steps being taken to make sure that all workers are treated well. Even once millions of new, skilled jobs have been created as part of an industrial strategy, the economy will still need 'elementary workers', such as cleaners, call-centre staff, distribution centre staff, security guards and delivery workers, who deserve to be treated with decency and respect.

Treating workers well shouldn't be regarded as exceptional behaviour, or something for businesses to boast about; it should be regarded as the norm. It is inexcusable and unnecessary that some workers are stuck in the kind of insecure, unpredictable jobs that mean they can't spend sufficient time with their families, in their communities or playing an active role in civic life. A lack of dignified or secure work produces what Matthew Taylor has described as a 'scarcity mindset, limiting people's horizons and imaginations, forcing them to focus on the here and now rather than longer term possibilities'.[10]

Having to juggle multiple jobs, working long hours and dealing with the childcare implications of last-minute shift changes have a clear impact on family life, health and stress levels. The fact that around 6 million working people are below the poverty line symbolises the growth of insecurity. People in the 'precarious' part of the economy should be entitled to the same levels of respect and decency as people who work in professional services, including a basic level of rights for all workers.

We shouldn't be hamstrung by copying the EU's Social Chapter, which, although obsessed about by many on the left, represents only the bare minimum of worker protection. Instead, the UK should seek to have the best workers' rights in Europe, enshrined within a workers' charter.

A new generation of workers, such as cleaners, security guards and those in call centres and distribution warehouses, have been let down by the failure of trade unions to show how they are relevant. This has meant that many of the people in the most insecure jobs are lacking representation in the workplace, and also in many cases lacking the kind of benefits many professional workers take for granted. The sight of elementary workers having to risk their lives during the Covid pandemic because of a lack of sick pay was an all too visible symbol that the lack of basic benefits is more than just a theoretical discussion.

Rather than maintain the present system, now should be the time to consider new forms of worker representation within these industries. Part of the present failure is the failure of unions to appeal to or represent people in a number of different industries dominated by low pay and poor conditions. If traditional unions aren't able to do this, then other structures should. Sectoral bargaining at a local level, sometimes through unions but also potentially through cooperatives or work councils directly elected by the workforce, could make a real difference to people's lives. Giving cleaners or distribution workers, for example, the power to negotiate as a sector would ensure decent standards for everyone in that field across a locality, whilst maintaining some flexibility and preventing a race to the bottom, with one company not able to undercut others over pay and conditions.

Sectoral bargaining would also enable workers and businesses to agree a minimum floor of rights, including on areas such as sick pay, paid holiday, pensions and basic certainty over hours. The fact that a 'race to the bottom' is ruled out means that firms are then more incentivised to differentiate through productive investment in their workforce, innovation and customer retention. Sectoral bargaining would also mean that a new generation of 'gig workers' could be included within the system. Labour MP Jon Cruddas has also proposed a number of important ideas to increase the societal importance of less-skilled work, including a special covenant for key workers, with additional entitlements to housing and travel. It is essential that we all look to ensure that work is always seen as fulfilling, secure and a source of dignity and respect. Measures to increase the dignity of unskilled work, the sense of control that low-paid workers have over their working lives and the ability for all workers to progress should be an important part of a new economic settlement.

8. Deepening the Partnership Between Workers and Businesses and Institutionalising It in Corporate Governance

An economic settlement that regards the economy as a partnership between workers, businesses and communities should mean that all jobs come with the kind of rewards and security that enable people to play a role in their local communities and spend time with their families. This should look to break the cycle where precarious employment also results in greater levels of stress and illness amongst low-paid workers. As figures as diverse as Clement Attlee and Marco Rubio have recognised, such a partnership should come with an understanding that both workers and businesses have rights and obligations: businesses have a right to make a profit but also an obligation to invest those profits in the workforce and productive investment; workers have an obligation to work but should also expect some of the profits they have helped generate to be reinvested in them. Too much of modern politics only views one side of this deal and ignores the other. A prosperous future requires both sides of the partnership to be acknowledged, and both sides to play their role.

The new settlement should look to restore some of the balance between capital and labour. It should look to create a productive capitalism, where business leaders are encouraged to innovate and grow companies and are rewarded for doing so, but where they also act in a partnership with workers to drive companies forward. The tax system should be used to encourage investment – such as in plant, machinery or R&D – and reward entrepreneurship, whilst not incentivising short-termist behaviour – such as share buybacks, exaggerated dividends or executive bonuses. Entrepreneurs should be saluted for their importance within the economy and rewarded for the risks they take. This partnership would mean workers are treated as long-term partners in the enterprise and are rewarded with a decent wage share of profit, improved investment and proper job security.

The partnership between businesses and workers should also be represented in how medium and large businesses are organised. A framework for a better organised, more dignified economy would include giving workers a seat at the table. We know that shareholder primacy theory incentives short-termist, quick returns, rather than the longer-term investment that our economy is in urgent need of. Conversely, worker representation on boards has been shown to help increase productivity, enhance retention and promote a longer-term focus. It would be a pivotal way of formalising the partnership between workers and employers. Worker representation on remuneration committees will also help to rein in the excesses of executive pay. Although Germany is the best example of a major country that requires worker representation on boards, it is also the case in countries such as Austria, the Netherlands and Sweden. Research has found that business investment is over 40 per cent higher in countries that have workers on boards.

The shift towards a partnership model has also found champions in what may, on the face of it, be surprising places. Andy Haldane, former chief economist at the Bank of England, has argued that society might 'require a rethink of the relative roles of capital and labour ... [The shareholder-led model] may not always make for the best outcomes, either for companies themselves or for wider society. And a further tilt in the balance of power in favour of capital could make that situation worse.'[11] Such unlikely institutions as the *Harvard Business Review* and McKinsey & Co. have made the case that a corporate governance that purely answers to shareholders is bound to fail, and that new models that take note of the interests of workers and communities will make for more effective systems.

Two elements in which people are being further left behind in a two-tier economy are housing and a lack of capitalisation. Put simply, the professional middle class are more likely to own shares and more likely to own houses. For many at the lower end of the income spectrum, capitalism without capital seems the order of the day. Encouraging companies to give capital to their employees, from middle managers to cleaning staff, would be an important first step towards fixing the disconnect between capital and wages. Beyond this, the growth of mutual and cooperative models, in which all workers in a company have ownership power, should be strongly encouraged. A government-led housebuilding scheme inspired by Macmillan's heroic efforts in the 1950s would also give more working people the power, freedom and dignity that comes with home ownership.

The role for government should clearly be creating an environment in which business can succeed and prosper, and in doing so to deliver benefits for communities, families and workers. Businesses should fulfil their share of the bargain, though, and large businesses should be reporting annually about how they are reinvesting profits in their broader workforce, whether that's through wages, equity, training or other productive investment. Government should ensure that regulatory incentives always promote longer-term investment and do not incentivise short-term punts. A move towards a model by which business treats its workforce as a partner will encourage longer-term thinking, provide greater agency to workers and help to tackle the UK's long-running issues around low-skilled work and low productivity.

9. Putting Vocation and Skill at the Heart of Our Education System

Our education system must be one that ensures everyone is able to make the most of their potential, whether that potential is achieved through academic or vocational

means. For decades, the education system has inadvert-
ently helped to widen the gulf between winners and losers
in the new economy. Resources have been concentrated
on the 50 per cent who go to university, and funding for
further education has been cut by governments of all parties. It is high time that the focus shifted to the 50 per cent
who don't go to university, to help ensure that the UK
does genuinely have the high-skill, high-wage economy
we often talk about.

A vicious, reinforcing cycle has been created whereby
elitism and snobbery are often based on levels of education, and the education system has failed to give an
adequate chance to people from poorer backgrounds. A
divide is clear even from the age of five and goes on getting
wider as children get older. As such, the divide, and what
Michael Sandel memorably described as credentialism, or
the prejudice of the highly educated towards the less well
educated, becomes self-reinforcing. Tackling educational inequality thus becomes an essential part of tackling
the inequality of respect and esteem that has become too
great a feature of British life. Although education reform-
ers of both parties have made real efforts to prioritise
improving education for poorer children, there is clearly
much more that needs to be done.

A comprehensive programme of education reform
should be based upon a simple and clear question: *Will
this change improve the life chances of young people from*

working-class backgrounds, and will it help narrow educational disparity and inequality of esteem?

A root and branch programme of educational reform needs to improve life chances from birth right through to retirement. As we've seen, people born in working-class communities are often already at a disadvantage by the time they turn five, and people in working-class jobs are much less likely to undertake in-work training or 'adult learning'. We also know that young people from working-class backgrounds are much more likely to become disengaged from the education system at an early age and more likely to attend a school rated 'poor' by Ofsted. They are also less likely to go to university (and this is particularly the case for white working-class boys), and those who don't make it to university are unlikely to be able to pursue vocational education that is regarded as on par with the academic equivalent. At each stage in the process, hurdles are placed in front of people from poorer backgrounds, and judgements are made about the same people who have faced lifelong obstacles. A pro-worker education policy should aim at removing these barriers and developing an education system that ensures nobody is left behind or ignored.

Equally, governments of all parties have invested in childcare, but more needs to be done to target that support where it is most badly needed. Parents shouldn't be penalised financially if they decide that they want to provide childcare at home, and quality childcare facilities, including potential for early years learning, should be located in those working-class communities where young people are already left behind by the age of five. Similarly, the goal of schools reform should be to dramatically increase the number of outstanding schools in those communities most impacted by educational inequality. This means doing whatever it takes to ensure the best teachers and headteachers are incentivised to teach in these schools for a reasonable amount of time, with a clear remit and substantial resources. Government should commit to narrowing the inequality in exam results within five years. Similarly, both universities and governments should take steps to narrow the gap that has left white working-class boys in particular educationally excluded.

The most substantial and important part of a pro-worker education policy, however, must be the revival and transformation of technical education. Whilst the expansion of higher education has helped more working-class people go to university, it has primarily helped even more middle-class people to go to university, with middle-class students still dominating the top institutions. Many poorer students who make university have ended up in lower-ranked universities, with degrees that have brought them little value in the jobs market. An obsession with higher education has also meant that those who don't attend university are regarded as 'failures', with technical education too often seen as the choice of those who have 'dropped out' or 'failed their exams'. Although the majority of the population don't have a degree, it has become fashionable to decry those without a degree as having failed.

Children who show academic promise are likely to have the system orientated around them from an early age, with the clear goal of them attending a good university. Children who show an aptitude for more practical tasks are unlikely to have either the time or support to help them develop their individual talents. Even for those of a young age, our education system is organised in a way that is almost designed to disengage and demoralise those who have strengths that aren't academic. As we've noted, this discouragement, exclusion and snobbery towards those without post-eighteen academic qualifications continues throughout their lives.

Such a one-eyed education policy risks wasting our natural talents, dividing the country and holding back the economy. The truth is that high-quality technical education is fundamental to the UK successfully reindustrialising, crucial for our future economic competitiveness and essential to narrow the snobbish divide that impacts too much of modern Britain. Developing a vocational offering that is genuinely the equal of the academic offer would truly be a transformational and positive step.

Reforms such as T-Levels and apprenticeships are

important steps, but more must be done to properly level the gap in esteem between technical and academic education. For too much of society, the snobbery that exists towards vocational education is a small-scale embodiment of the snobbery that exists in the rest of society. They like the *idea* of vocational education but regard it as for 'other people'. The gulf in esteem won't be fully bridged until politicians, business leaders and professionals are delighted to see their children go on to technical education and Parliament has as many graduates of our vocational education institutions as it does of our old universities.

A vocational education system that is a match for Germany and Scandinavia will need an immense amount of ambition, as well as the clear engagement of businesses, workers, communities, colleges and universities. We know that quality technical education doesn't come cheap and will need considerable investment in equipment, skilled teachers and up-to-date facilities. Further education colleges have had funding cut for decades as resources became concentrated in academic education; that trend needs to be reversed.

At the age of thirteen or fourteen, just when the most catastrophic disengagement from our current system tends to begin, young people should be given the option of pursuing a vocational or an academic route, with regular opportunities to switch routes. Those who choose the new route would be given extensive technical instruction, as well as a placement at an employer and a continuing education in core academic subjects. At sixteen, they could then go on to beefed up T-Levels or become part of the National Apprenticeship Scheme before potentially taking a vocational post-eighteen qualification. In all cases, this would be combined with increasingly intense employer placements. Providing an account for lifelong learning for those who choose the vocational route is also an option that should be given serious consideration.

Courses would be designed in partnership with employers and trade unions and would also be seen as an integral part of the active industrial strategy that we must pursue, with important industries of the future being strongly represented. The partnership that should be at the centre of the economy should also be at the core of the new generation of vocational education: business should be incentivised to invest in state-of-the-art specialist centres, just as Nissan is developing its centre for automotive engineering in Sunderland. The funding regime should also be levelled, with young people choosing the vocational route having access to similar levels of support as those pursuing an academic one. Strengthening the National Apprenticeship Scheme, the running of which should be devolved at a local level with some labour market entry reserved for apprentices, would also be an important step towards recognising vocation. Such a scheme could be largely devolved to a local level and run in cooperation between trade unions, chambers of commerce, local colleges, universities and other stakeholders – who would be able to design the scheme based on local needs and also consider which roles should be ringfenced for apprentices only.

10. Building Strong and Active Communities

The societal divide that has helped create the new snobbery can also be seen physically in differences in the public realm. Whereas many metropolitan cities (and London in particular) have benefited from glittering regeneration projects, new art galleries and museums and deeply impressive city-centre renewal, many towns were left to decay. Infrastructure spending was highest in London and the south-east (with success becoming a self-fulfilling cycle) and lowest in those areas that needed the investment the most.

Although major cities do have pockets of poverty, they also have access to large amounts of social, and economic, capital, which is not replicated in post-industrial communities. Important hubs of community engagement, from pubs and post offices to theatres and working men's clubs, have declined. Areas of shared community space, such as high streets, parks, and football and cricket clubs, have fallen into disrepair or been lost completely. In the past two decades, a quarter of all pubs, a quarter of all Post Offices and a fifth of all libraries have closed. Youth services, parks and leisure centres also saw substantial cuts during the years of austerity. People in post-industrial towns are angry at how the physical space in their towns has been left to decline and at how their high streets have lost their department stores and become littered with bargain shops, bookies and travel agents.

Declining social capital has also been accompanied by a rise in social and health problems, including drug addiction, alcoholism and depression. People in deprived areas are six times more likely than those in prosperous areas to die of alcohol-specific liver disease. The so-called Red Wall seats have lower life expectancy than other parts of the country. Tackling the disengagement, which is partially driven by a sense of lack of pride and esteem in work and in communities, must be a real priority. It is crucial that rebuilding a sense of dignity and place in the local community goes alongside rebuilding esteem and growth in local economies.

The sense of ownership and engagement that must run through political transformation must ultimately run through to ensuring stronger and more empowered communities. The social fabric, which in many places has been hit by industrial decline, must be restored and the ability for active citizenship revived. Communities and local economies that have often been shelled out must be revitalised. Prioritising a real sense of economic security, decent local jobs and dignified work will on their own enable people to play an active role in their local community, but they must also be combined with a strenuous effort to give people power in their local communities. Rebuilding strong civic institutions built around a sense of local identity, enduring physical infrastructure and high-quality shared public space will all be important.

Giving real power to local authorities and providing them with the resources to build recovery would be an important step in achieving this. An element of levelling up has concentrated on distributing funds from a central pot. This is an important approach, but the most transformative approach should come from giving communities the power, the resources and the skills to revive themselves, and the scope to experiment and innovate. Rebuilding institutional capacity within local authorities and giving greater power to cities, counties and towns would be a useful first step. For decades, the skills of local authorities have been cut back, with councils' powers being reduced, local authorities being urged to embrace outsourcing and national firms utilising 'economies of scale' to provide services. Whilst this might have had rationale in terms of cost-cutting, it has reduced the potential of local authorities to have a strong local skillset, decreased their ability to coordinate local improvement and diminished the accountability of local services. Restoring the importance of a lifelong and skilled career and increasing state capacity at a local level will help enable local authorities to take the lead in the rebuilding of social capital. Of course, this shouldn't all be done by local bureaucrats. What commentators like Julian Le Grand and Andrew Laird have described as the hybrid economy, which encourages local authorities, communities, philanthropists and businesses to work together to strengthen local regeneration and community facilities, also has an important role to play in ensuring that local people can access the resources they need to improve community services.

Devolution of power to local authorities should only be the first step in a more substantial change. Ultimately, it is communities themselves that should be given greater power, impetus and drive; rather than the central government dictating what change and revival looks like in local communities, it should be those areas that are able to draw on the resources of central government to fulfil local change. The relocation of Treasury jobs within Treasury North in Darlington is a good start, but there needs to be a rethink of the way Whitehall as a whole operates. They should, in many ways, become providers of support and expertise to local communities and local authorities, as well as acting as the base for sharing lessons from local experiments and building a national plan for levelling up from local initiatives. Whitehall should exist to serve local communities, rather than the other way round.

Empowering local authorities should be accompanied by measures to galvanise communities at a neighbourhood or even street level to enhance their local area. Digital technology provides the tools for much more direct citizen engagement in key decisions and a much more active citizenry. This means local people should feel they have ownership of the decisions that impact them in their local community – decisions are made *with* them rather than being imposed.

In addition, resources should be provided to communities looking to deliver change in their local area, and part of this should be focused on providing places where people can come together with a shared feeling of place and belonging. As Tory MP Danny Kruger has argued, community improvement districts should be introduced to allow community-led innovation in bespoke areas, and a 'community right to serve' should give people the power to run some local services themselves. High streets and town centres shouldn't just be places people go to shop; as is the case in France, they should be communal spaces where communities and families come together.

As well as incentivising philanthropic initiatives, the government should also support measures to help save or revive important institutions, such as local football teams, cultural institutions and green space. Institutions that encourage people to gather and share public areas, from pubs to libraries, should also be supported. Government should provide support to help pubs diversify into wider-ranging community facilities and should dramatically cut beer duty so that drinking in a local pub is always cheaper than buying alcohol in a supermarket. Libraries should also be supported as important community hubs which also encourage knowledge-sharing and digital inclusion.

Locally owned businesses also bring real value to neighbourhoods and help boost community pride. Maintaining such a locally owned presence should be essential. Micro businesses have also been an important part of building stronger community ties during lockdown, but they risk being strangled by excessive bureaucracy. Encouraging local businesses both through cutting red tape on community micro businesses and through enabling local banks to provide a source of finance could together promote an upsurge in local community businesses.

As James Frayne and Andy Westwood have both argued, a 'local identity strategy' might be an important part of rebuilding relationships and communities at a local level. Even before larger-scale regeneration or change, merely making efforts to improve the physical look and feel of communities will be important. And as Rachel Wolf suggests, the small things, like hanging baskets, are important and give people renewed pride in their area. Reviving local transport infrastructure is also crucial, and whilst rail and tram links cannot be improved overnight, local bus services can. Similarly, reviving community events, such as annual shows, markets, firework displays and sporting competitions, can increase a sense of belonging.

The institutions that matter locally aren't just the pub and the library. An obsession towards 'big is better' has removed the communal bonding institution of the village or town school. Cutbacks in the police have meant many communities lack a local police presence, and people feel less safe in their local community. Both of these are negative developments. Boosting police resources so communities have a familiar and visible police presence would also play an important part in strengthening communities.

Taking measures to strengthen the social fabric is an essential part of the new settlement that needs to be built, and empowering local people to guide and make decisions that will impact them is also crucial. Just as working people should be empowered in the economy, it is also important that they are empowered in their local area, knowing that change will be steered by them, rather than happen to them.

An Empowered and Active Working Class

Recent decades have seen the gradual disempowerment of working people, with them being elbowed out of centres of economic, cultural and political power. This disempowerment has been matched by the rise of a new snobbery, with lower societal esteem for working-class occupations and prejudice against those with fewer qualifications being regarded as socially acceptable in some quarters. The 2016 referendum represented working Britain shouting 'enough is enough', and the 2019 election saw those same voters demanding that, after decades of being ignored, their voice must be heard this time. We must deliver a new economic and political settlement that responds to that demand and meets the urgency of the moment. As we have set out, this can only be done by a relentless focus on decent, dignified work and restoring power to working people in politics, in the workplace and in their communities.

ACKNOWLEDGEMENTS

Thank you to my parents, George and Lynda, for their constant support and encouragement.

Enormous thanks to everyone who has reviewed, and doubtless improved, chapters and offered thoughts and guidance.

Thanks to Andrew Laird, Anthony McDonald, Anthony House, Ben Furnival, Ben Winch, Craig and Joan Barnett, David and Sue Furnival, Dom Goggins, Ed Taylor, Frank Strachan, Helen Bowman, James Bloodworth, James Probert, Jason Cowley, Jim Curry, Jon Cruddas, John McDonald, Luke Maynard, Matthew Goodwin, Maurice Glasman, Nadhim Zahawi, Nicklas Lundblad, Nick Faith, Nick Timothy, Penny Mordaunt, Phil Boorman, Richard Holden, Rony Yuria, Samuel Kobes, Sanghyun Lee, Seb Payne, Simon Cawte, Steve Akehurst, Steve Brister, Ted Osius, Tim Shipman and Tom Mauchline, among others.

I appreciate the time provided by people in Singapore,

South Korea and Taiwan who have shared their thoughts and their expertise.

Particular appreciation to Olivia Beattie, Lucy Stewardson, Vicky Jessop and the team at Biteback for putting faith in this book and guiding me through the process.

NOTES

INTRODUCTION: THE BIRTH OF THE NEW SNOBBERY

1 'It's time for the elites to rise up against the ignorant masses', Foreign Policy, 28 June 2016.
2 British Social Attitudes Survey 33, 2016.
3 Benjamin Butterworth, 'Jeremy Corbyn "couldn't lead the working class out of a paper bag", Alan Johnson says after exit poll result', i, 13 December 2019.
4 'Dawn Butler: "If anyone doesn't hate Brexit – even if you voted for it – there's something wrong with you"', Turning Point UK, 13 December 2019.
5 Terry Christian, tweet, 10.16 a.m., 4 May 2021, https://twitter.com/terrychristian/status/1389509343222157312
6 Dan O'Hagan, tweet, 7.07 a.m., 7 May 2021, https://twitter.com/danohagan/status/1390548709537157121; Alex Green, tweet, 9.12 a.m., 7 May 2021, https://twitter.com/GlexAreen/status/1390580177378463745

CHAPTER ONE: THE POLITICAL MARGINALISATION OF THE WORKING CLASS

1 Adrian Zorzut, 'Labour MP brands Brexiteers "absolute sh*tbag racist w*nkers" during Rule Britannia row', New European, 26 August 2020.
2 Rachel Wearmouth, 'Labour should ignore voters who "hate blacks, women and gays", says Paul Mason', HuffingtonPost, 29 May 2019.
3 Engels to Marx, written on 18 November 1868.
4 Rajeev Syal, 'Disproportionate number of Labour's new members are wealthy city dwellers', The Guardian, 21 January 2016.
5 Quoted in Thomas Frank, The People, No (New York: Henry Holt & Co., 2020).
6 'Educationalism and the irony of meritocracy: negative attitudes of higher educated people towards the less educated', Journal of Experimental Social Psychology (2018), vol. 76, pp. 429–47.
7 'How Britain voted in the 2016 EU referendum', Ipsos MORI, 5 September 2016.
8 Paul Collier, 'Take back control', The Spectator, 23 February 2019.
9 Dambisa Moyo, 'My plan to save democracy', The Guardian, 2 May 2018.
10 Tim Shipman, All Out War (London: Harper Collins, 2016).
11 'Skegness's Jolly Fisherman redrawn by New European', BBC News, 13 April 2017.

12 'Vince Cable provokes backlash after saying those who voted for Brexit are "driven by nostalgia" and long for a world where "faces are white"', *The Independent*, 12 March 2018.

13 Jessica Simor QC, tweet, 1.53 p.m., 27 February 2021, https://twitter.com/JMPSimor/status/1365661259920773120

14 Quoted in James Andrews, 'All the shops reopening their doors to customers today – including Primark', *Daily Mirror*, 15 June 2020.

15 'Labour MP blasts "fat old racists" amid row over BBC move to use orchestral version of Rule Britannia at the Proms', PoliticsHome, 26 August 2020.

16 Maurice Glasman, 'All hail good King Boris', UnHerd, 20 December 2019.

17 Deborah Mattinson, 'Five things Labour should do to win back the red wall', *The Times*, 21 September 2020.

18 'Election Review foreword: key findings and summary recommendations', Labour Together, 2019.

19 Thomas Frank, *Listen, Liberal: Or, Whatever Happened to the Party of the People* (London: Scribe Publications, 2016).

20 Interview with *Newsweek*, 1970.

21 Paul Mason, 'Corbynism is over – Labour's next leader must unite the centre and the left', *New Statesman*, 13 December 2019.

22 Engels to Marx, 18 November 1868.

23 Lee Harpin, 'Unite members furious with McCluskey after *Panorama* interview', *Jewish Chronicle*, 6 August 2020.

24 See Simon Heffer, 'Rise of the new working-class Tories', *New Statesman*, 22 January 2020 and the headlines from a number of Tory-supporting newspapers post-election.

25 Foundation statement of the Labour Representation Committee, 1900.

26 Richard Ekins, 'The Case for Reforming Judicial Review', Policy Exchange, 2020.

27 Lord Dyson, 'Is Judicial Review a Threat to Democracy?', Sultan Azlan Shah Lecture, 2 December 2015.

28 'Elitist Britain 2019: the educational backgrounds of Britain's leading people', Sutton Trust, 2019.

29 Jeff Goldsworthy, 'Losing faith in democracy: why judicial supremacy is rising and what to do about it', Policy Exchange, 9 March 2015.

30 Jonathan Rayner, 'Class warrior: interview with David Greene', *Law Society Gazette*, 19 February 2018.

31 'Quangos "unaccountable, confused and neglected" says MPs' report', Public Sector Executive, 10 November 2014.

32 Michael Pinto-Duschinsky and Lynne Middleton, 'Reforming public appointments', Policy Exchange, 2013.

33 David Gauke, 'I fear the Conservative Party is lost for small state free marketeers and One Nation social liberals', ConservativeHome, 4 July 2020.

CHAPTER TWO: EXCLUDED: THE CULTURAL AND EDUCATIONAL ROOTS OF THE NEW SNOBBERY

1 T. S. Eliot, *Notes Towards the Definition of Culture* (London: Faber & Faber, 1973).

2 Speech in Llandudno, May 1987.

3 James Callaghan, 'A rational debate based on the facts', Ruskin College Oxford, 18 October 1976.

4 'Poorer Children's Educational Attainment', Joseph Rowntree Foundation, 2010, p. 5. The report goes on to say, 'Young children from the poorest fifth of families are ranked on average at around the thirty-fourth percentile at the age of

three. This is around twenty-three percentage points lower than the average rank among the richest fifth of children. This rich–poor gap has risen to nearly twenty-seven percentile points by the time the children have reached the age of five.'

5   Ofsted Annual Report 2012/13.
6   'Underachievement in education by white working-class children', House of Commons Education Committee, 11 June 2014.
7   Quoted in Chris Snowden, 'The lost boys: the white working class is being left behind', *The Spectator*, 18 July 2020.
8   Discussion with Legatum Institute to launch Hand, Head, Heart.
9   Michael Shiner and Philip Noden, '"Why are you applying there?": "Race", class and the construction of higher education "choice" in the United Kingdom', *British Journal of Sociology of Education* (2015), vol. 36, no. 8, pp. 1170–91.
10 'Social class in higher education: still an elephant in the room', *Routledge Handbook of the Sociology of Higher Education* (Oxford: Routledge, 2016).
11 'State of The Nation 2018–19: social mobility in Great Britain', Social Mobility Commission.
12 Catriona Paisey, Nick Paisey, Heather Tarbert and Betty (H. T.) Wu, 'Deprivation, social class and social mobility at Big Four and non-Big Four firms', *Accounting and Business Research* (2020), vol. 50, no. 1, pp. 61–109.
13 'Funding for 16–19 education routes', Education Policy Institute, May 2019.
14 Quoted in 'Why aren't we talking about further education and social mobility?', Education Data Lab, 13 November 2015.
15 'State of the Nation'.
16 Mattha Busby, 'Durham student rugby team forced to cancel event mocking miners' strike', *The Guardian*, 26 November 2017.
17 Nazia Parveen, 'Students from northern England facing "toxic attitude" at Durham University', *The Guardian*, 19 October 2020.
18 Ibid.
19 'State of the Nation'.
20 Sam Friedman and Daniel Laurison, *The Class Ceiling: Why It Pays to Be Privileged* (Bristol: Bristol University Press, 2019).
21 Joan C. Williams et al., 'Why Companies Should Add Class to Their Diversity Discussions', *Harvard Business Review*, 5 September 2018.

CHAPTER THREE: THE RISE OF 'WOKE' AND THE MARGINALISATION OF WORKING-CLASS CONCERNS

1   Jeremy Bohonos, 'Critical race theory and working-class white men', *Gender, Work and Organization* (2020), vol. 28, no. 1.
2   Mason, 'Corbynism is over'.
3   David Brooks, 'The problem with wokeness', *Seattle Times*, 8 June 2018.
4   Helen Pluckrose and James Lindsay, *Cynical Theories: How Activist Scholarship Made Everything About Race, Gender and Identity – And Why This Harms Everybody* (North Carolina: Pitchstone Publishing, 2020), p. 12.
5   Rory Tingle, 'Outrage as controversial taxpayer-funded black studies professor who says Britain is "built on racism" claims Churchill was "a white supremacist" in debate', *Daily Mail*, 12 February 2020.
6   Dan Falvey, 'Oxford lecturer doesn't want UK to find coronavirus vaccine due to political correctness', *Daily Express*, 24 April 2021.

7   Edward Said, 'A window on the world', *The Guardian*, 2 August 2003.
8   Trevor Phillips, 'When you erase a nation's past, you threaten its future', *The Times*, 18 September 2020.
9   Craig Simpson, 'Churchill college panel claims wartime PM was a white suprem-acist leading an empire "worse than the Nazis"', *Daily Telegraph*, 11 February 2021.
10 'Keele manifesto for decolonizing the curriculum', *Pluto Journals* (2018), vol. 5, nos 1–2, pp. 97–9.
11 See the 'Decolonise Education' section of the NUS website.
12 Gurminder K. Bhambra et al., *Decolonising the University* (London: Pluto Press, 2018), p. 64.
13 Eugenia Cheng, *X+Y: A Mathematician's Manifesto for Rethinking Gender* (London: Profile Books, 2020).
14 Sandra Grey, 'Activist academics: what future?', *Policy Futures in Education* (2013), vol. 11, no. 6, p. 708.
15 Prof. Kalwant Bhopal, tweet, 11.45 a.m., 28 November 2020, https://twitter.com/KalwantBhopal/status/1332651736021012486
16 Kimberlé Crenshaw, 'Mapping the margins: intersectionality, identity politics, and violence against women of color', *Stanford Law Review* (1991), vol. 43, no. 6.
17 Pluckrose and Lindsay, *Cynical Theories*.
18 Harry Mount, 'The rise of the Econian', *The Spectator*, 1 August 2020.
19 Helen Lewis, 'The world is trapped in America's culture war', *The Atlantic*, 27 October 2020.
20 George Packer, 'Face the bitter truth', *The Atlantic*, 4 November 2020.
21 Nesrine Malik, '"I've had to fight": Kehinde Andrews on life as the first UK profes-sor of Black studies', *The Guardian*, 4 February 2021.
22 Trevor Phillips, 'The march of wokeism is an all-pervasive new oppression', *The Times*, 6 November 2020.
23 Charles Reich, *The Greening of America*, quoted in Frank, *The People, No*.
24 Scott Galloway, tweet, 2.13 a.m., 6 November 2020, https://twitter.com/profgalloway/status/1324535357854126082
25 Aris Roussinos, 'Is cosmopolitanism our destiny?', UnHerd, 13 October 2020.
26 Robin DiAngelo, *White Fragility* (Boston: Beacon Press, 2018), pp. 132–3.
27 John McWhorter, 'The dehumanizing condescension of *White Fragility*', *The Atlantic*, 15 July 2020.
28 E. Cooley, J. L. Brown-Iannuzzi, R. F. Lei and W. Cipolli, 'Complex intersections of race and class: Among social liberals, learning about White privilege reduces sympathy, increases blame, and decreases external attributions for White people struggling with poverty', *Journal of Experimental Psychology: General* (2019), vol. 148, no. 12, pp. 2218–28.
29 Sally Weale, 'White working-class pupils suffering due to "status deficit", MPs told', *The Guardian*, 13 October 2020.
30 Kevin D. Williamson, 'Chaos in the family, chaos in the state: the white working class's dysfunction', *National Review*, 17 March 2016.
31 Alec MacGillis, 'The Original Underclass', *The Atlantic*, 16 September 2016.
32 Phillips, 'The march of wokeism'.
33 'Bari Weiss's *New York Times* resignation letter in full', *The Times*, 14 July 2020.
34 'A letter on justice and open debate', *Harper's*, 7 July 2020.
35 Michael Lind, 'The Revenge of the Yankees', *Tablet*, 16 November 2020.

CHAPTER FOUR: A CULTURE OF SNOBBERY?

1 Kevin Rawlinson, 'Julie Walters: lack of working-class actors is sad', *The Guardian*, 23 January 2015.

2 Christian Hewgill, 'We got a lot of grief when our photo became a meme', BBC News, 18 January 2021.

3 'Death of elderly Brexit voters could change second EU result, Ian McEwan claims', *The Independent*, 13 May 2017.

4 *Sunday Telegraph*, quoted in Tony Thorne, *Dictionary of Contemporary Slang* (London: A & C Black, 2007).

5 James Delingpole, 'A conspiracy against chavs? Count me in', *The Times*, 13 April 2006.

6 James Frayne, 'Ten errors that Conservatives must avoid making about the new working-class voters who backed them last month', ConservativeHome, 21 January 2020.

7 Rawlinson, 'Julie Walters: lack of working-class actors is sad'.

8 Stephen Armstrong, 'Ant and Dec's war on media elitism: "TV is too London-centric – we want to change that"', *Daily Telegraph*, 5 May 2021.

9 Rachel Deeley, 'British fashion exploits, celebrates and fetishises the working class', *Business of Fashion*, 17 September 2019.

10 Sean O'Hagan, 'Gary Hume: I couldn't hold down a job. That's why I became an artist', *The Guardian*, 18 May 2013.

11 Stuart Maconie, 'The privileged are taking over the arts – without the grit, pop culture is doomed', *New Statesman*, 4 February 2015.

12 Anita Singh, 'Where are the BBC's working-class presenters, asks Michael Buerk', *Daily Telegraph*, 26 March 2019.

13 Roy Greenslade, 'Here's how to make the media fit for modern Britain', *The Guardian*, 7 July 2019.

14 'Panic! Social class, taste and inequalities in the creative industries', Arts and Humanities Research Council, 2018.

15 Matthew Moore, 'Metropolitan mindset is alienating BBC viewers, says Tim Davie', *The Times*, 17 September 2020.

16 *Today*, BBC Radio 4, 4 April 2017.

17 'The Oxbridge white bloke's day is over at the BBC, says comedy controller', *The Independent*, 19 June 2018.

18 Anita Singh, 'BBC cancels *The Mash Report*, show criticised for "left-wing bias"', *Daily Telegraph*, 12 March 2021.

19 Roger Mosey, 'Bowing to Twitter culture is bad news for the BBC', *The Times*, 19 July 2020.

20 Mark Townsend, 'John Humphrys attacks BBC's "liberal bias" days after retiring', *The Guardian*, 21 September 2019.

21 Mosey, 'Bowing to Twitter'.

22 Jim Waterson, 'Jon Snow cleared by Ofcom over "white people" comment', *The Guardian*, 5 August 2019.

23 'Waitrose is on the march against Brexit – but what of Lidl Britain', *The Guardian*, 22 October 2018.

24 Rod Muir, 'Jon Snow can't remember if he chanted "f*ck the Tories" at Glastonbury', Total Politics, 27 June 2017; '*Channel 4 News* boss says media have right to call politicians "liars"', BBC News, 22 August 2019; Jamie Doward, '"Back off", controversial professor urges critics of Channel 4's Cathy Newman', *The Guardian*, 21 January 2018.

25 *Daily Telegraph*, 14 June 2008.

26 'Panic!', Arts and Humanities Research Council.

27 James Heale and Chris Hastings, 'Outrage at BBC Horrible Histories Brexit show for "trashing Britain" with song that says "your British things are from abroad and most are stolen" on day UK left EU', *Mail on Sunday*, 1 February 2020.

28 'The Londoner: I'm not afraid of "kill whitey" joke critics, says Sophie Duker', *Evening Standard*, 21 October 2020.

29 Craig Simpson, 'Exclusive: British Library's chief librarian claims "racism is the creation of white people"', *Daily Telegraph*, 29 August 2020.

30 Adam White, 'British Museum removes bust of slave-owning founder Sir Hans Sloane: "We have pushed him off the pedestal"', *The Independent*, 25 August 2020; 'Let's create: strategy 2020–2030', Arts Council England; David Sanderson, 'Staying neutral impossible after Black Lives Matter, says National Gallery chief', *The Times*, 3 November 2020; Craig Simpson, 'William Hogarth out of favour as British cartoon museum says its displays are over-represented by "white, cisgender men"', *Daily Telegraph*, 13 December 2020; 'Tate vision 2020–25', The Tate; Jack Malvern, 'Kew Gardens plant signs will acknowledge links to slavery', *The Times*, 11 March 2021.

31 'Britain's choice: common ground and division in 2020s Britain', More in Common, October 2020.

CHAPTER FIVE: WHAT ABOUT THE WORKERS?
THE TWO-TIER ECONOMY THAT UNDERPINS THE NEW SNOBBERY

1 Lisa Mckenzie, '"We don't exist to them, do we?" Why working-class people voted for Brexit', LSE Blogs, 15 January 2018.

2 Michael Sandel, *The Tyranny of Merit: What's Become of the Common Good* (London: Penguin, 2020).

3 'Executive pay in the FTSE 100, 2020 review', CIPD, August 2020.

4 'Addressing employer underinvestment in training', CIPD, July 2019.

5 'Margaret Thatcher interview for *The Sun*', 28 February 1983.

6 Francis Wheen, 'Satirical fiction is becoming Blair's reality', *The Guardian*, 14 February 2001; Patrick Wintour, 'Gordon Brown: Middle class to be our election battleground', *The Guardian*, 15 January 2010; Patrick Wintour, 'David Cameron presents himself as leader of "aspiration nation"', *The Guardian*, 10 October 2012; 'A first glimpse of Theresa May's meritocracy vision', *Financial Times*, 9 September 2016.

7 Kwame Anthony Appiah, 'The myth of meritocracy: who really gets what they deserve?', *The Guardian*, 19 October 2018.

8 B. Lopes, C. Kamau and R. Jaspal, 'The roles of socio-economic status, occupational health and job rank on the epidemiology of different psychiatric symptoms in sample UK workers', *Community Mental Health Journal*, 6 March 2018.

9 James Bloodworth, *The Myth of Meritocracy: Why Working-Class Kids Still Get Working-Class Jobs* (London: Biteback, 2016).

10 Sandel, *The Tyranny of Merit*, p. 26.

11 F. A. Hayek, *The Constitution of Liberty* (Oxford: Routledge, 2006).

12 Michael Young, 'Down with meritocracy', *The Guardian*, 29 June 2001.

13 Quoted in Wheen, 'Satirical fiction is becoming Blair's reality'.

14 Patrick Deneen, 'A Tyranny Without Tyrants', *American Affairs*, 20 February 2021.

15 Sandel, *The Tyranny of Merit*.

16 David Goodhart, 'Middle May: the premier is one of the first to recognise Britain's emerging political fault line', *The Spectator*, 20 May 2017.

17 Quoted in 'Classic podium: the Tories' historic mission', *The Independent*, 2 October 1998.
18 Quoted in Jonty Bloom, 'The European Coal and Steel Community turns sixty', BBC News, 10 August 2012.
19 Aditya Chakrabortty, 'Why doesn't Britain make things any more?', *The Guardian*, 16 November 2011.
20 JJ Charlesworth, tweet, 5.40 p.m., 14 October 2020, https://twitter.com/jjcharlesworth_/status/1316418588207648774
21 'Covid-19: low-skilled men have highest death rate of working age adults', *BMJ* (2020), no. 369; 'Coronavirus related deaths by occupation, England and Wales: deaths registered between 9 March and 28 December 2020', ONS, 25 January 2021.
22 'You can't buck the market', *The Independent*, 5 April 1998.
23 'Tony Blair's conference speech 2005', *The Guardian*, 27 September 2005.
24 'Gordon Brown's Mansion House speech', *The Guardian*, 22 June 2006; 'Gordon Brown – 2007 Mansion House speech', Political Speech Archive.
25 *The Observer*, 18 October 2008.
26 'Pope Francis: Politics cannot be "slave" to economy, finance', The Hill, 24 September 2015.
27 Quoted in David Goodhart, 'How to make low-skilled jobs seem more attractive', BBC News, 17 February 2013.
28 Jonathan Cribb, 'How are younger generations faring compared to their parents and grandparents', Institute for Fiscal Studies, 17 October 2019.

CHAPTER SIX: BEYOND THE SECESSION OF THE SUCCESSFUL
1 Jonathan Swift, *The Conduct of Allies*, quoted in Susan Ratcliffe (ed.), *Oxford Essential Quotations* (Oxford: Oxford University Press, 2016).
2 Interview with Matt Forde, 'Show 192 – Deborah Mattinson returns', *Political Party* [podcast], 11 December 2020.
3 Sir John Major speech, quoted in 'Sir John Major: do more to boost social mobility', *The Guardian*, 11 November 2013.
4 Glasman, 'All hail good King Boris'.
5 Benjamin Disraeli, *A Vindication of the English Constitution*, quoted in Peter Viereck, *Conservative Thinkers* (Oxford: Routledge, 2006).
6 Clement Attlee, 'Leader's speech, Scarborough', 1951.
7 Robert F. Kennedy, 'Remarks at the University of Kansas', 18 March 1968.

CONCLUSION: RESTORING DIGNITY, ESTEEM AND POWER: TEN STEPS TO BUILDING A PRO-WORKER SETTLEMENT
1 Walter Benn Michaels, *The Trouble with Diversity: How We Learned to Love Identity and Ignore Inequality* (New York: Henry Holt & Co., 2007).
2 'Transforming the BBC', BBC Diversity and Inclusion Plan, 2021–2023.
3 *Financial Times*, 21 July 2009.
4 Alastair Stewart, 'Battle of Orgreave: A bloody battle which transformed industrial relations', ITV News, 31 October 2016.
5 'The return of the policy that shall not be named: principles of industrial policy', IMF, March 2019.
6 Azeem Azhar, 'New thinking is needed on workers' rights', *The Economist*, 17 November 2020.
7 'The return of the policy that shall not be named', IMF.

8 Ibid.
9 'Labour markets: riding high in a workers' world', *The Economist*, 10 April 2021.
10 Matthew Taylor, 'An age of insecurity', RSA, 20 November 2019.
11 Andrew Haldane, speech to TUC, 'Labour's share', 12 November 2015.

INDEX